Alone on a Wide
Wide Sea

MICHAEL MORPURGO is one of Britain's best-loved writers for children, and was recently awarded an OBE in the Queen's 80th Birthday Honours List for his services to literature. He has written over 100 books and won many prizes, including the Smarties Prize, the Whitbread Award and the Writers' Guild Award. In 2005 he won the Blue Peter Book Award for his novel *Private Peaceful*, which was also adapted into a stage play by the Bristol Old Vic and has been toured to great acclaim.

From 2003 to 2005 Michael was the Children's Laureate, a role which took him all over the UK to promote literacy and reading, and in 2005 he was named the Booksellers Association Author of the Year.

Michael lives in Devon with his wife Clare. Both have been awarded MBEs for their work in founding the charity *Farms for City Children*.

'Michael Morpurgo's name on a book is a guarantee of quality.' *Daily Telegraph*

Alone on a Wide Wide Sea

michael morpurgo

HarperCollins *Children's Books*

To Lula Léa and Clare, who helped make this book with me.

My thanks to Alex Whitworth and Peter Crozier, mariners extraordinaire
and quite ancient too, whose emails while circumnavigating the world in their
yacht Berrimilla in 2004 informed and inspired this story. Thanks also to
Graham Barrett and Isabella Whitworth for all their wonderful help and
encouragement. And of course I mustn't forget Samuel Taylor Coleridge...

First published in hardback in Great Britain by HarperCollins *Children's Books* 2006
First published in paperback in Great Britain by HarperCollins *Children's Books* 2007
HarperCollins *Children's Books* is a division of HarperCollins*Publishers* Ltd
77-85 Fulham Palace Road, Hammersmith, London W6 8JB

This edition produced 2011 for
The Book People, Hall Wood Avenue, Haydock, St Helens, WA11 9UL

The HarperCollins Children's Books website address is
www.harpercollins.co.uk

2

ISBN-13 978-0-00-790966-7

Printed and bound in England by
Clays Ltd, St Ives plc

Contents

Part One

The Story of Arthur Hobhouse

Part Two

The Journey of the Kitty Four

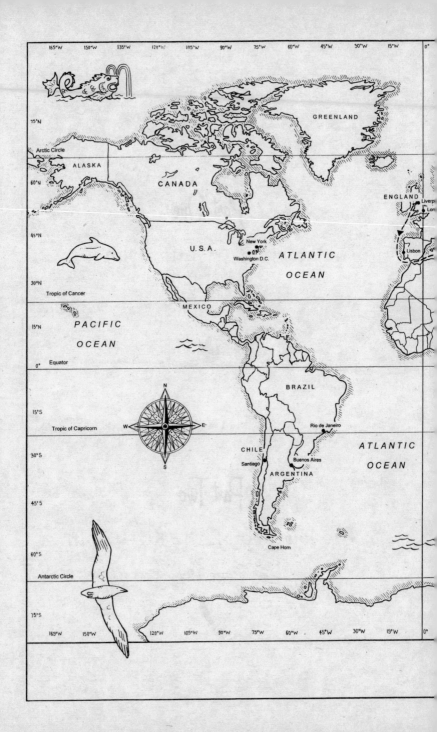

Part One

The Story of
Arthur Hobhouse

Arthur Hobhouse
is a Happening

I should begin at the beginning, I know that. But the trouble is that I don't know the beginning. I wish I did. I do know my name, Arthur Hobhouse. Arthur Hobhouse had a beginning, that's for certain. I had a father and a mother too, but God only knows who they were, and maybe even he doesn't know for sure. I mean, God can't be looking everywhere all at once, can he? So where the name Arthur Hobhouse comes from and who gave it to me I have no idea. I don't even know if it's my real name. I don't know the date and place of my birth either, only that it was probably in Bermondsey, London, sometime in about 1940.

The earliest memories I have are all confused somehow, and out of focus. For instance, I've always known I had a sister, an older sister. All my life she's been somewhere in the deepest recesses either of my memory or my imagination – sometimes I can't really be sure which – and she was called Kitty. When they sent me away, she wasn't with me. I wish I knew why. I try to picture her, and sometimes I can. I see a pale delicate face with deep dark eyes that are filled with tears. She is giving me a small key, but I don't remember what the key is for. It's on a piece of string. She hangs it round my neck, and tells me I'm to wear it always. And then sometimes I hear her laugh, an infectious giggle that winds itself up into a joyous cackle. My sister cackles like a kookaburra. She comes skipping into my dreams sometimes, singing *London Bridge is Falling Down*, and I try to talk to her, but she never seems to be able to hear me. Somehow we're always just out of reach of one another.

All my earliest memories are very like dreams. I know that none of them are proper memories, none that I could really call my own anyway. I feel I've come out of half-forgotten, half-remembered times, and I'm sure I've often filled the half-forgotten times with made-up memories. Perhaps it's my mind trying to make some sense of the unknown. So I can't know for certain where the made-up ones end and the real ones begin. All the earliest childhood memories must be like that for everyone I suppose, but maybe mine are more blurred than most, and maybe that's because I have no family stories to support them, no hard facts, no real evidence, no certificates, not a single photograph. It's almost as if I wasn't born at all, that I just happened. Arthur Hobhouse is a happening. I've been a happening for sixty-five years, or thereabouts, and the time has come now for me to put my life down on paper. For me this will be the birth certificate I never had. It's to prove to me and to anyone else who reads it that at least I was here, that I happened.

I am a story as well as a happening, and I want my story to be known, for Kitty to know it – if she's still alive. I want her to know what sort of a brother she had. I want Zita to know it too, although she knows me well enough already, I reckon, warts and all. Most of all I want Allie to know it, and for her children to know it, when they come along, and her children's children too. I want them all to know who I was, that I was a happening and I was a story too. This way I'll live on in them. I'll be part of their story, and I won't be entirely forgotten when I go. That's important to me. I think that's the only kind of immortality we can have, that we stay alive only as long as our story goes on being told. So I'm going to sit here by the window for as long as it takes and tell it all just as I remember it.

They say you can't begin a story without knowing the end. Until recently I didn't know the end, but now I do. So I can begin, and I'll begin from the very first day I can be sure I really remember. I'd have been about six years old. Strange that the memories of youth linger long, stay vivid, perhaps because we live our young lives more intensely. Everything is fresh and for the first time, and unforgettable. And we have more time just to stand and stare. Strange too that events of my more recent years, my adult years, are more clouded, less distinct. Time gathers speed as we get older. Life flashes by all too fast, and is over all too soon.

Three Red Funnels
and an Orchestra

There were dozens of us on the ship, all ages, boys and girls, and we were all up on deck for the leaving of Liverpool, gulls wheeling and crying over our heads, calling goodbye. I thought they were waving goodbye. None of us spoke. It was a grey day with drizzle in the air, the great sad cranes bowing to the ship from the docks as we steamed past. That's all I remember of England.

The deck shuddered under our feet. The engines

thundered and throbbed as the great ship turned slowly and made for the open sea ahead, the mist rolling in from the horizon. The nuns had told us we were off to Australia, but it might as well have been to the moon. I had no idea where Australia was. All I knew at the time was that the ship was taking me away, somewhere far away over the ocean. The ship's siren sounded again and again, deafening me even though I had my hands over my ears. When it was over I clutched the key around my neck, the key Kitty had given me, and I promised myself and promised her I'd come back home one day. I felt in me at that moment a sadness so deep that it has never left me since. But I felt too that just so long as I had Kitty's key, it would be lucky for me, and I would be all right.

I suppose we must have gone by way of the Suez Canal. I know that most of the great liners bound for Australia did in those days. But I can't say I remember it. There's a lot I do remember though: the three pillar-box-red funnels, the sound of the orchestra playing from first class where we weren't allowed to go – once they even played *London Bridge is Falling Down* and I loved that because it always made me happy when I heard it. I remember mountainous waves, higher than the deck of the ship, green or grey, or the deepest blue some days, schools of silver dancing dolphins, and always, even in the stormiest weather, seabirds skimming the waves, or floating high above the funnels. And there was the wide wide sea all around us going on it seemed to me for ever and ever, as wide as the sky itself. It was the wideness of it all I remember, and the stars at night, the millions of stars. But best of all I saw my first albatross. He flew out of a shining wave one day, came right over my head and looked down deep into my eyes. I've never forgotten that.

The ship was, in a way, my first home, because it was the first home I can remember. We slept two to a bunk, a dozen or more of us packed into each cabin, deep down in the bowels of the ship, close to the pounding rhythm of the engines. It was cramped and hot down there and reeked of diesel and damp clothes, and there was often the stench of vomit too, a lot if it mine. I was in with a lot of other lads all of whom were older than me, some a lot older.

I was in trouble almost from the start. They called me a "softie" because I'd rock myself to sleep at night, humming *London Bridge is Falling Down*, and because I cried sometimes. Once one of them found out I wet my bed too, they never let me forget it. They gave me a hard time, a lot of grief. They'd thump me with pillows, hide my clothes, hide my shoes. But sending me to Coventry was the worst, just refusing to speak to me, not even acknowledging my existence. I really hated them for that. They reserved this particular punishment for when I was at my most miserable, when I'd been sick in the cabin.

Sea-sickness was my chief dread. It came upon me often and violently. To begin with I'd do what everyone else seemed to do, I'd vomit over the rail – if I could get there in time. It was while I was doing this one day that I first met Marty. We were vomiting together side by side, caught one another's eye, and shared each other's wretchedness. I could see in his eyes that it was just as bad for him. It helped somehow to know that. That was how our friendship began. Some kindly sailor came along and took pity on us both. He gave us some advice: when it gets rough, he told us, you should go below, as far down as you can go. It's the best place, because down there you don't feel the roll of the ship so much. So that's what we did, and it worked – mostly. Marty came down to my cabin, or I'd go to his. But sometimes I'd get caught out and find myself having to be sick on the cabin floor. I'd clean it up, but I couldn't clean up the smell of it, so if I'd done it in my cabin they'd send me to Coventry again. It was to avoid having to face them that I sought out Marty's company more and more. I think it was because I felt safe with him. He was a fair bit older than me, about ten he was, older even than the boys in my cabin and taller too – the tallest of all of us, and tall was important. I never asked him to protect me, not as such. But I knew somehow he might, and as it turned out, he did.

We were up on deck, the two of us, watching an albatross gliding over the waves – like me, Marty loved albatross – when a gang of these lads from my cabin were suddenly there behind us. They were northern lads, all of them – sometimes I could hardly understand what they said. One of them, their ringleader Wes Snarkey, started calling me names and taunting me, I can't remember why. I was "nowt but a poxy cockney!" Marty stared at Wes for a moment. He just walked right up to him and knocked him flat. One punch. Then he said very quietly, "I'm a cockney too." They all slunk away, and after that life got a whole lot easier for me down in the cabin. It might have been just as hot and sticky, just as crowded and smelly, but at least they more or less left me alone. All Marty's doing.

It was Marty too who explained it all to me – why we

were on the ship, where we were going and why. I don't know how much, if anything, I had understood before. We were going to Australia, that was all I knew for certain. All of us, Marty said, had been specially chosen from all the orphans in England to go out and live in Australia – that's what he'd been told. Australia, he said, was a brand new country where there hadn't been a war, where there hadn't been bombings and rationing, where there was lots of food to eat, huge parks to play in, and beaches too. We'd be able to go swimming whenever we liked. I told him I couldn't swim, and he said he'd teach me, that I'd soon learn. And, he explained, we weren't ever going to be sent to an orphanage again like the ones we'd grown up in, but instead we were all going to live in families who wanted to look after us. So, with all that to look forward to, it was worth being sea-sick for a while, wasn't it? Nothing was worth being sea-sick for, I said, and I promised I would never ever set foot on a ship or a boat again, not for all the tea in China. It was a promise I singularly failed to keep – often.

During that whole long voyage into an uncertain future, Marty cheered my spirits. He became like a big brother to me, which was why I confided in him about Kitty, about how she'd been left behind and how much I missed her. I showed him the lucky key she'd given me. I could never think of her or even say her name without crying, but Marty never seemed to mind me crying. But he *did* mind me humming *London Bridge is Falling Down*, said I was always doing it, and couldn't I hum another tune? I said I didn't know any others. He told me that, like as not, Kitty would probably be coming out to Australia on another ship, that there wasn't room on this one, which was why they hadn't let her on, that I'd see her again soon enough. That was Marty through and through, always hopeful, always so certain things would work out. But Marty, as I discovered later, didn't just hope things would get better, he'd do all he could to make sure they did too.

You need people like Marty just to keep you going. Even if things don't seem to be working out quite as you'd like them to, you need to feel they're going to, that all will be well in the end. If you don't believe that, and sometimes in my life I haven't, then there's a deep black hole waiting for you, a black hole I came to know only too well later on. I learned a lot from Marty on that ship, about hope, about friendship. Mighty Marty everyone called him, and it was a nickname that suited him perfectly.

Kookaburras, Cockatoos and Kangaroos

In my time I've sailed into dozens of harbours all over the world. None is more impressive than Sydney. Liverpool had been grim and grey when we left, Sydney was blue and balmy and bright and beautiful. It was an arrival I shall never forget. We came in to port in the morning in our grand red-funnelled ship, the ship's horn sounding to announce us proudly. And I felt part of all this new glory.

Marty and I stood there leaning on the ship's rail, gazing

in wonder – *agog* is the best word for it, I think. Everything about the place was new and marvellous to me, the warmth of the breeze, the hundreds of sailing boats out in the bay, white sails straining, the majesty of Sydney Harbour Bridge, the red-roofed houses on the hillsides all around, and the sea – I never knew blue could be so blue. Nowhere could have been more perfect. I knew without question that we were steaming into paradise. And as the ship crept in, ever closer, I could see that everyone was waving up at us and smiling. We waved back. And Marty put his fingers in his mouth and whistled. I was filled with sudden hope. I was aglow with happiness, and so was Marty. He had his arm around my shoulder. "I told you, Arthur, didn't I?" he said. "A brand-new country. We'll be all right now."

In all the bustle and chaos on the dockside they gathered all of us children together, gave us a roll call, and then, without telling us why, began to split us up into groups. When I saw what was happening I stayed as close to Marty as I could. The last thing I wanted was to get separated from him. But that's just what they tried to do. Marty grabbed my arm, held on to it, and told me to stay right where I was beside him. Quick as a flash, he said, "Him and me, Mister, we're cousins. Where Arthur goes, I go. Where I go, Arthur goes." The man ticking our names off his list said it was quite impossible, that arrangements had already been made and couldn't be changed. He was adamant, and bad-tempered too. He shouted at Marty to button his lip and do as he was told. Like everyone else on the dockside, he spoke English, but it didn't sound the same language as it had in England at all. I recognised the words, some of them, but the sounds they made were different and strange.

Marty didn't shout back and scream. He didn't jump up and down. Marty, I discovered, had his own very individual way of dealing with authority. He spoke very quietly, perfectly politely, fixing the man with a steady stare. "We're staying together, Mister," he said. And we did too, which was why I found myself later that morning sitting beside Marty on a bus, heading out of Sydney and into open country. There were ten of us on that bus, all boys, and as I looked around me I was relieved to see that only one of the boys from my cabin was there. It was Wes Snarkey, the one Marty had thumped that day on deck – he'd never given me any trouble since, so that didn't bother me. Lady Luck really had smiled on me – that's what I thought at the time anyway.

The driver, who seemed a chatty, cheerful sort of bloke, told us he was taking us to Cooper's Station, a big farm over 300 miles away. It would take us all day to get there. Best to settle down and sleep, he said. But we didn't. None of us did. There was too much to look at, too many wonders I'd never seen before. For a start, there were the wide open spaces, hardly a house in sight, hardly any people either. But that wasn't all that amazed me that first day in Australia. All the animals and birds were as different and strange to us as the country itself. The bus driver told us what they were – and it turned out their names were about as odd as they were themselves – kookaburras and cockatoos and kangaroos and possums. They didn't even have the same trees we had back home in England. They had gum trees and wattle trees instead. This wasn't just a different country we were in, it was more like a different planet. And the scrubby surface of this planet seemed to go on and on, flat on every side as far as the horizon, which shimmered blue and brown and green. And the towns we drove through were like no towns I'd seen before. They had great wide dusty streets, and all the houses were low. If you saw another car it was a surprise.

I was hot and dusty and thirsty on that bus, and I

thought the journey would never end, but I was happy. I was happy to have arrived, happy not to be sea-sick any more. Tired though we were, we were buoyed up by the excitement of it all. This was a new adventure in a new world. We were on a bus ride into wonderland and we were loving it, every single moment of it.

Evening was coming on by the time we got to Cooper's Station, but we could still see enough. We could see it was a place on its own, way out in the bush, and we could tell it was a farm. I mean you could smell it straightaway, the moment we clambered down off the bus. There were huge sheds all around, and you could hear cattle moving and shifting around inside. And from further away in the gloom there was the sound of a running creek, and ducks quacking raucously. A gramophone record was playing from the nearby farmhouse, which had a tin roof and a verandah all around it. I thought at first that was where we'd all be living, but we were led past it, carrying our suitcases, down a dirt track and into a compound with a fence all around. In the centre of this was a long wooden shed with steps at one end and a verandah.

"Your new home," the man told us, opening the door. I didn't take much notice of him, not then. I was too busy looking around me. The gramophone needle got stuck as I stood there. I can never think of Cooper's Station without that stuttering snatch of a hymn repeating itself remorselessly in my head, "What a friend we have in Jesus, have in Jesus, have in Jesus, have in Jesus". I wasn't to know it then, but it was the eerie overture that heralded the darkest years of my life.

Cooper's Station and
Piggy Bacon and God's Work

I think it was from the moment they first shut us in the dormitory block at Cooper's Station, and we heard the door bolted behind us, that I have hated walls about me and locked doors. I never lock the doors of my house even now – never. Ever since Cooper's Station, doors and walls have made me feel like a prisoner. I was about to find out, as we all were, not what it was *like* to be a prisoner, but what it *was* to be a prisoner. Worse still we were slaves too.

I've had a lot of time to think things over since. I'm still angry about Cooper's Station, about what they did to us there. But we weren't the first. Two hundred years or so before we were sent out from England to Australia, others had made the same journey we did. They had come in chains in the stinking bowels of transport ships. We may have come in a beautiful ship, with pillar-box-red funnels and an orchestra, but we were prisoners just like them. And they must have very soon discovered, as we did, that you weren't just a prisoner, you were a slave as well, and that when you're a slave they don't just take away your freedom, they take away everything else as well because they own you. They own you body and soul. And the soul, we were about to find out, was particularly important to our owners.

I can't pretend I had any understanding of all this then, lying there clutching my lucky key in the sweltering darkness of the dormitory during my first night at Cooper's Station, but I knew already that the dream had died. Marty lay in the bunk next to me, stunned to silence like the rest of us. He cried that night, the only time I ever heard Marty cry. I knew now this brand-new country we had come to was not a paradise after all. It was, as we were soon to discover, a hell on earth – a hell specially devised for children by Mr Bacon, Piggy Bacon we called him, who was to be our gaoler, slave-master, preacher and brand-new father, all in one.

I can honestly say that Piggy Bacon was the only person in all my life that I ever wanted to kill. But to be fair to him, he did at least tell it to us straight. That first morning at Cooper's Station, after washing from the buckets lined up out on the verandah, after our breakfast of lukewarm, lumpy porridge, he told us exactly why we were there. We were all gathered there shivering outside the dormitory block. Mrs Bacon was at his side in her blue dungarees and flowery apron, tiny alongside his great bulk. He was a great thickset bull of a man, red-faced with short, cropped ginger hair and a clipped ginger moustache, and little pink eyes – even his eyelashes were ginger. He always seemed to me like a man on fire and about to explode. His vast stomach looked as if it was only just held in by his checked shirt and broad belt, a belt every one of us would have good cause to fear as the months passed. He wore knee-length boots which he'd whack irritably from time to time with the stick he used to carry – the same stick he would use for punctuating his speeches – speeches which, like this one, always turned into sermons. Sometimes he'd carry a whip for cracking at the dogs, at the cattle or the horses, or us if he felt like it. Stick or whip, it didn't matter to us – we came to fear both just as much.

Mrs Bacon smiled the same fixed nervous smile that day that I so often saw afterwards. We didn't know the reason she was nervous, not then. She seemed shrunk inside her dungarees – I think she always wore the same blue dungarees, only the aprons changed. I sensed from the first that Mrs Bacon was frightened, that she was hiding something. Her face was drained of all colour. I never in my life saw a woman look more weary. She stood there, her eyes downcast, as Piggy Bacon told us all the whys and wherefores, the do's and don'ts of Cooper's Station.

"You can count yourselves very lucky," he began, "that Mrs Bacon and I have taken you in. No one else would, you know. We did it out of the kindness of our hearts, didn't we, Mrs Bacon? Out of the kindness of our hearts, that's what it was. You are the little ones no one else wanted. You are the little ones thrown out of the nest, rejected and with no home to go to, no one to look after you, no one even to feed you. But we will, won't we, Mrs Bacon? We will feed you and house you, we will clothe you and teach you about hard work and the ways of God. What more could a child ever want? Mrs Bacon and I are God fearin' folk, Christian folk. We were brought up to know our duty. 'Suffer little children to come unto me,' the good Lord said. So we are doing his will, and this we shall train you to do as well. A child is born sinful and must be bent to the will of God. That is now our task.

"So we have offered to take you in, at our own expense mind, out of good Christian charity. We have built you this home for your shelter – your shelter from the storm of life. You will help us make a garden of Eden, a paradise out of this wilderness. Mrs Bacon and I will be like a mother and father to you, won't we, Mrs Bacon? And your training in the ways of the Lord will begin right now. There will be no swearing, no idleness – I promise you, you will be kept too busy ever to be idle. You will work to earn your keep. And you will work because the Devil makes work for idle hands. If you work we shall feed you well. If you work well you may play for one hour at the end of each day, the last hour before sundown.

"Look out there!" he roared suddenly, waving his stick towards the horizon. "Look! Do you see? Nothing. Nothing but wilderness as far as the eye can see, and that nothing goes on for miles and miles north, south, east and west. So don't you ever think of running off. You'd go round in circles out there. You'd die of thirst, be shrivelled up by the sun. The snakes would bite you, the crocs would eat you up, or the dingo dogs would tear you to pieces. And even if you survived all that, the black fellows would soon find you – they always do what I say – and they'd just bring you right back here to Cooper's Station. Isn't that right, Mrs Bacon?"

Mrs Bacon did not respond. She just stayed there beside him, eyes still lowered, while he ranted on.

When she thought he'd finished she walked away towards the farmhouse, followed closely by her dun-coloured dog, a furtive frightened creature like his mistress, who slunk along behind her, his tail between his legs. But Piggy Bacon had not finished, not quite. He glared after her, and then slapped his boot with his stick. "It's God's work we're doing," he said. "God's work. Always remember that."

And so to God's work we went.

Suffer Little Children

Piggy Bacon kept his promise to us faithfully: he did indeed always keep us too busy ever to be idle. From that day on anything that needed doing on the farm we children did it. We were the slaves that tried to carve his paradise out of the wilderness for him. The work was either smelly or back-breaking and often both at the same time. There were thirty milk cows and their calves and a hundred bullocks or more on that station. We fed them, watered them, drove them, cleaned up after them. And before long we were milking the cows too. I ached from my fingers to my shoulders with the work of it. Then there were Piggy Bacon's chickens – he had hundreds of them – and his pigs and his horses too.

Mornings were spent mostly refilling the wash buckets from the pump, shovelling muck, wheeling it out to the dung heap from the calf sheds, or spreading it on the paddocks. And always the flies found you, every fly in Australia. They were all around you, in your eyes, in your hair, up your nose even, and they were biting ones too. And if you swallowed one – and you often did – you'd try to retch it up, but you never could. We couldn't escape them any more than the animals could.

Lunch was soup and bread brought to our long trestle table in the dormitory and ladled out into our bowls by Mrs Bacon, who scarcely ever spoke to us. We lived on soup and bread in that place. Then in the afternoons we'd be set to clearing the paddocks of stones, or we'd be fetching and carrying water to the troughs, and blocks of salt too. These buckets almost pulled my arms out of my sockets they were so heavy. You had to fill them right up too, because if ever Piggy Bacon caught you carrying a half-empty bucket you were in big trouble, and trouble always meant the strap. So we filled them up full to the brim every time. And when all the water-carrying was done, we'd be digging up weeds or filling in potholes in the tracks, or pulling out tree roots, all of us straining together on the ropes.

Our hands blistered, our feet blistered. Bites and sores festered. None of that mattered to Piggy Bacon. Once one job was done there was always another waiting. We worked hard because he'd stop our food just like that if we didn't. We worked hard because he'd strap us if we didn't. We worked hard because if we didn't he'd cancel our evening playtime and make us work an hour extra at the end of the day. I so longed for that hour off – we all did – and we hated to miss it. That promise of an hour's playtime was what kept me going when every bone in my body ached with tiredness.

Feeding up the animals was the last task of the day, the only work I really enjoyed. Chickens, cows, pigs, horses – it didn't matter – I loved to see them come running when they saw us with our sacks of feed. I loved to watch them loving it. But the milking I never liked. My fingers couldn't cope. They swelled easily and I couldn't sleep afterwards for the pain. Marty and I – we always tried to be in the same work party – would feed a few by hand if we could, if Piggy Bacon wasn't around to catch us. The chickens tickled you when they pecked the corn out of your hand, and the horses' noses felt warm and soft as they snuffled up their feed – you had to watch out in case they snuffled up your fingers as well.

There was one horse in particular Marty and I loved more than all the others. He was huge, a giant of a horse, shining black all over except for one white sock. Big Black Jack he was called, and whenever we were lucky enough to get to feed him, Marty and I made sure he had all the food and water he needed, and then some. I'd crouch there by his bucket, watching him drink deep, listening to his slurping, laughing at his dribbling when he lifted his head out of the bucket. I'd sing *London Bridge is Falling Down* to him, and he'd like that. He was Piggy Bacon's plough-horse, and Piggy treated him just as he treated us, worked him to the bone, till his head hung down with exhaustion. Horses, I discovered, when they're tired or sad, sigh just like people do. Big Black Jack used to do that often. We'd look one another in the eye and I'd know just how he felt and he'd know just how I felt too.

Whatever job we were doing, whenever we were out on the farm, we could be sure Piggy Bacon would turn up sooner or later. He would appear suddenly, out of nowhere. He only ever came for one reason, and that was to pick on someone for something. Each time I hoped and prayed it was someone else he'd pick on. But sooner or later my turn would come around. We either weren't working fast enough, or hard enough. A water bucket wasn't full enough, or he'd find a field stone we hadn't picked up – any excuse would do. He wouldn't strap us there and then. Instead he'd tell us how many whacks the particular crime merited and then give us all day to think about it. That was the torture of it, the waiting.

The punishment parade would take place in the evening outside the dormitory hut just before supper and before we were locked in for the night. He'd call you out in front of the others and then pronounce sentence on you just like a judge. And you'd stand there, hand outstretched, trembling and tearful. It happened to all of us, and often. No one escaped it. But Marty got it more than most, and you could see that when Piggy Bacon strapped Marty he did it with real venom. There was a good reason for that: Marty's look.

It was the same look he'd used on that officious man on the dockside the first day we landed in Australia. The thing was that Marty would never be cowed. He would look

Piggy Bacon straight in the eye, and that always set Piggy Bacon into one of his terrible rages. The rest of us kept our heads down, just tried to keep out of trouble. Marty fought back with silent defiance. And he didn't cry out like I did, like the rest of us did, when we were strapped – he wouldn't give him the satisfaction. He just stood there unflinching, his jaw set, his eyes stoney, no tears, no trembling. And to add insult to injury, he'd say thank you afterwards too, his voice as stony as his stare. I'd like to say we all took heart from that, but we didn't. We admired him though – everyone did. But he wasn't the only one who fought back. We soon had another hero to admire, a most unlikely hero too – Wes Snarkey.

Wes Snarkey's Revenge

Neither Marty nor I had ever much liked Wes, and Wes made it quite obvious he didn't much like us either. I could never forget how he and his cronies had tormented me almost every night on the ship, and I'm sure he could not forget how Marty had come to my defence and humiliated him on the deck that day. That must still have rankled with him. So the result was that we hardly ever spoke. In fact he hardly ever spoke to anyone during those first months at

Cooper's Station. In the dormitory, at the line of wash buckets on the verandah, eating at the long trestle table, out at work on the farm, he kept himself to himself. Even at evening playtime when we'd all be kicking a football around, he'd sit there on his own, gazing out at nothing. Of all of us Wes Snarkey was the only loner. But then one day I found out that he wasn't really a loner at all. He had a friend – a best friend.

Time and again Piggy Bacon had strapped him for wandering away from his work. No one knew where he went and he didn't tell anyone. One moment he'd be there digging a ditch alongside you, the next he'd be gone. Strapping Wes didn't stop him from sneaking off, so I knew that whatever he was doing, wherever he was going, must have been really important to him. We were mucking out the pigs one day when I noticed he'd gone off again. I made quite sure Piggy Bacon wasn't about, and went looking for him. I found him by Big Black Jack's paddock. I crouched down behind the trunk of a fallen gum tree and watched him. He was standing by the fence, feeding Big Black Jack with some bread crusts, and he was talking to him as if he was a real person, not a horse at all. I was close enough to see everything, and to hear everything too.

Wes was telling him about a horse he'd known in England, in Leeds, a milkman's horse, a piebald mare she was, and how every morning he'd sit on the wall of the orphanage in the early morning and wait for her to come, how he'd save his bread crusts to feed her, how one day the milkman had let him sit on her, and they'd gone off down the street, how it was the best day of his life. "Will you let me ride you one day, Jack?" he whispered, smoothing his neck. "Would you? I could ride you out of here and we'd never come back."

I must have shifted then or maybe it was a gust of wind that rustled the pile of dead leaves where I was crouching. Whatever it was, Wes turned around and saw me there. We stared at one another, not speaking. I could see he had tears in his eyes, and on his face too. He brushed them away hurriedly with the back of his hand then ran off before I could say anything. And I was going to say something. I was going to say that I liked Big Black Jack too, that we could be friends now if he wanted.

As it happened it was only a few days later that Wes Snarkey became everyone's friend, and that was on account of Piggy Bacon and his whip. Down near the creek, which was dried up for most of the year, there was an old tree stump we couldn't pull out. We'd been digging around it, and trying to pull it out for a whole day. With all of us hauling on the ropes, and even with Piggy Bacon lending a hand himself – and that hardly ever happened – we still couldn't shift it. So in the end Piggy Bacon harnessed up Big Black Jack and got him to do the job instead. But no matter how hard Jack strained at the ropes, the stump would not budge. Piggy Bacon shouted at him, but it did no good. Big Black Jack was doing all he could, we could see that. Piggy Bacon took a stick to him then, and whacked him again and again. He was bellowing at him.

"Useless bag of bones! Lazy devil! You good-for-nothing, you!" Then Piggy Bacon used his whip on him. In a frenzy of fury and frustration he whipped him till he bled. That was when Wes Snarkey went for Piggy Bacon.

He ran at him, screaming like a wild thing, head-butted him full in the belly, knocking the wind out of him and sending him sprawling in the dust. They rolled over and over with Wes ending up on top, sitting astride him and pounding him with his fists. And we were all cheering then and leaping up and down, until Mrs Bacon came running out from the house and pulled Wes off him, but not before the damage had been done, not before blood had been drawn.

Piggy Bacon was never quite as frightening to us again after that. His temper could still be terrifying, and we still hated him just as much. But we had seen the wicked giant felled. We'd seen his blood. He made Wes pay of course. He made us all pay. We had no playtime for a week, and no bread with our soup for a week either. Wes got twelve strokes of the strap that night and didn't seem to mind a bit. He sat on his bunk nursing his hand afterwards grinning up at us, looking happy as Larry. He knew he'd made new friends of all of us, and he was happy. So were we. From that day on there was a solidarity among us. We smiled more. We joked more. All this had been Wes Snarkey's doing. He'd had his revenge and it was sweet revenge for us all. He wasn't just a friend now, he was our hero too.

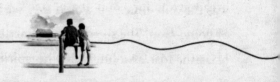

Saints and Sinners

Sunday at Cooper's Station was the only day we didn't have to work. We sang hymns and psalms, said our prayers and heard sermons instead. They went on all morning, outside the dormitory usually or inside if it was wet – which wasn't often. Piggy would stand on a box and harangue us with his sermons in between the hymns. Mrs Piggy, as we'd all come to call her, standing dutifully at his side, her dog lying at her feet fast asleep and twitching in his dreams, which broke the monotony of it. It was a welcome distraction and gave us something to nudge one another and wink about.

Mrs Piggy would play the squeezy box to accompany the hymns, and would sing out, her voice surprisingly strong, leading us all, her eyes closed in fervent concentration. This was the only time you would ever see her confident and full of conviction. She seemed to be carried away on the wings of faith, lost absolutely in the spirit of the hymns. Her piping voice rang out passionate with belief. After every hymn, she would cry out at the top of her voice: "Alleluia! Praise the Lord!" Then she'd lower her head and at once shrink back inside her shell, inside the Mrs Piggy we all knew, timid and tired and terrified, as Piggy Bacon launched into yet another thunderous sermon about the saints above and the sinners below, by which he meant us, about devils and hellfire and damnation. Through it all the dog slept blissfully. We just wished we could do the same.

But we weren't the only ones at the Sunday services. This was the only day the Aboriginal people, who lived in the country round about and who sometimes came to work on the farm – the "black fellows" Piggy called them – were allowed to come near the house. We'd see them often enough, the children mostly, when we were out on the farm, just crouching there in the distance watching us. Or sometimes we'd catch sight of a group of them moving through a heat haze on the horizon, not walking at all, it seemed to me, but rather floating over the ground. If ever they wandered in too close Piggy Bacon would go after them on his horse and drive them away with his whip, calling them all thieves and drunkards. But on Sundays Mrs Piggy invited them in for cakes and prayers. Even then they didn't like to come too close, but they'd squat down at a safe distance from us to listen to the hymns and sermons.

Afterwards Mrs Piggy would go over to them carrying a tray of cakes and lemonade, and she'd make the sign of the cross on their foreheads and bless them. None of us had seen that many black faces before, just an occasional one passing by in a London street perhaps, and I'd noticed one or two black American GIs in uniform driving around in jeeps back home. These people went barefoot in ragged clothes and their children ran about naked, and they made you feel uncomfortable because they seemed always so still as they squatted there scrutinising you, their dark eyes looking right into yours. They stared. We stared. But we hardly ever spoke. You could never tell what they were thinking. But I liked having them there. They were company. And in this desolate place of wide skies and wide horizons, where we saw so few people, just their presence was a comfort.

Hardly anyone besides them ever came to Cooper's Station. A truck coming down the long farm track was a real event for us, because it was that rare, maybe one or two a week, that's all – delivering animal feed, or fencing wire, or seed perhaps. The drivers often sat on the verandah and drank lemonade with Piggy and Mrs Piggy. They had cakes too. We got cakes and lemonade only on Sundays, our big treat of the week, one each with a cherry on the top. We'd line up and Mrs Piggy handed one to each of us. She'd bless us and sign a cross on our forehead too. I liked that. It was the only time she ever touched us. I always took the cherry off my cake, put in my pocket and kept it till last. Sometimes I'd keep it until I was in bed, and I'd lie there letting it melt slowly in my mouth, my hand grasping my lucky key all the time.

They tried to make us say our prayers at night. We'd all have to kneel there for ten minutes in silence. I never prayed, but I did wish. Every night, clutching the key around my neck, I wished myself out of there, wished myself back home in England, back with Kitty.

In that first year, like everyone else, I almost found myself liking Mrs Piggy, and not just because of her Sunday cakes either – though that certainly had something to do with it. The truth was I felt sorry for her, we all did. And in a way I suppose she had our respect too. Unlike Piggy Bacon himself, she worked as hard out on the farm as we did. She milked the cows with us in the morning and evening, and she made all our meals too. The porridge and the soup and bread and the milky puddings may have been repetitious and tedious, but it was hot and it was regular. And Mrs Piggy did it all.

Then there were the good days, the only good days, when Piggy Bacon drove off in his truck into town, and we'd be left alone on the farm just with her. We still had our work to do, but she'd do it with us. And on these rare and happy days you'd see all the tension and the exhaustion lift from her shoulders, and even hear her laugh sometimes. We were the same. Without Piggy Bacon there, we could fool around, have fun! On those days she was a different person.

But every time it would be over all too soon. Unlike her

there was some refuge for us, together in our locked dormitory at night. We had each other too. She still had Piggy Bacon. Sometimes, the worse for drink, he'd throw things at her – you could hear the sound of smashing crockery in the farmhouse. You'd hear him shouting at her, hitting her too, beating her. I never saw it happen, but we heard it.

"Don't you dare tell me how to treat them! I'll do what I like and how I like, you hear me woman?" He'd go on and on at her.

We'd lie there listening, and the next morning we'd see the bruises. So in time we began to feel she was one of us, just as much Piggy Bacon's slave as we all were. I've often wondered why she endured it, why she stayed with him. There's really only one answer that makes any sense at all: for the love of God, for Jesus' sake. I never knew a more devout woman than Piggy Bacon's wife. She was married to him in the eyes of the Lord, so she could never leave him. As we were to discover, she was a woman who didn't just believe, she really *lived* her faith, and she suffered for it too.

I only once caught a glimpse of the depth of her suffering. Marty and Wes and I had been told by Piggy to go and dig over their vegetable patch behind the farmhouse. It was a hot and humid afternoon. The flies were out and at us, and the soil was dried hard and unyielding. We'd been at it for hours, and we'd had enough. It was Marty's idea to have a rest and get ourselves a drink. Marty's ideas were often dangerous. But by now we were beyond caring, and anyway Piggy Bacon had just been round on one of his random patrols. We thought Mrs Piggy was out working on the farm somewhere. We dropped our forks and ran to the water pump outside the backdoor of the farmhouse. We pumped out the water for each other, all of us taking our turns to lie on the ground underneath, letting it splash all over our faces, drinking our fill. I was just having my turn, revelling in the coolness of it, when Marty and Wes stopped pumping. When I protested they shushed me, and then crept off, doubled up, along the side of the farmhouse. I could hear Mrs Piggy now, she was crying her heart out. I followed them. When they stood up to peek in at the window I did too. Standing on tip-toe I could only just see.

She was sitting there, rocking back and forth in her chair by the stove, her dog on her lap. On the table near us by the window were all the Sunday cakes she'd made. She was trying to stop herself sobbing by singing. It was very soft, but we could hear it well enough to recognise it: *What a friend we have in Jesus.* Verse after verse she sang, but punctuated always by fits of sobbing that wracked her whole body. There was one moment when she lifted her eyes and cried out loud: "Why, sweet Jesus? Why? Please take this cup from me, Jesus. Please take it." That was when I saw the purple bruise on her chin, the livid marks on her neck and some blood on her lip too. She was clasping her hands and praying. I remember thinking then that I wanted Piggy Bacon dead, that one day I would kill him. I never made actual plans to do it of course, but I felt like doing it, and so did Marty, and Wes too.

What he did next could so easily have made a murderer of me, if I'd had the means, if I'd had the courage, if circumstance hadn't intervened.

Mrs Piggy to Ida

It was Christmas time – our second Christmas on the farm
– about eighteen months or so after we arrived at Cooper's
Station. For lunch on Christmas Day, Piggy Bacon and Mrs
Piggy sat at opposite ends of our long trestle table and ate
with us. We'd had the day off – in all we were given three
days off in the year: Piggy Bacon's birthday, Easter Sunday
and Christmas Day. The morning had been all carols and
prayers, and of course sermons too, just like a normal

Sunday, except that I liked the carols a lot better than some of the dreary hymns we usually sang. We had sausages and mashed potatoes and gravy, and then jam roly-poly and custard afterwards, and all the lemonade we wanted. The best feast of my childhood; I've never forgotten it. With Piggy and Mrs Piggy there we none of us of said a word, of course, none of us dared. But I don't think any one of us wanted to talk much anyway – we were all far too busy eating our fantastic feast to have any time at all for conversation. We were savouring every mouthful. Ever since that Christmas Day I've always loved sausages.

It happened after the meal. As usual one of us had to stand up and say grace, not just before but after each meal as well. It happened to be my turn that day, and Piggy Bacon made me say it all over again because I'd mumbled it. "Say it loud to the Lord," he told me, "and he will hear you." So I did. Then he stood up himself, cleared his throat and announced that they had decided to give us each a Christmas present, "A gift from the Lord," he said, a gift that we could keep with us and treasure all our lives. Then he showed us what it was. Dangling there from his forefinger on a piece of cord was a small wooden cross. "From now on every one of you will wear this every day.

This is the badge of Jesus and you will wear it with pride," he said.

One by one we were summoned up to receive our present. He hung a cross around each of our necks. We said thank you, shook his hand and went to sit down again. Except for the thank yous the whole ceremony was conducted in an awkward silence. Mrs Piggy, who was standing meekly at his side with a bunch of crosses hanging from her wrist, handed a cross to him as each of us came up. I noticed she kissed each one before she gave it to him. Then I was called up. I was standing there waiting for my cross, looking up into Piggy Bacon's face, when suddenly his whole expression altered. "What's this?" he roared, and lunging forward he grabbed my key from around my neck and with one violent pull jerked it off.

"That's mine," I cried, reaching out to grab it back. He held it out of my reach, examining it, puzzling over it.

"A key? What for? A key to what?"

"It's my lucky key," I told him. "Kitty gave it to me, my sister in England."

"Luck!" Piggy Bacon thundered. "Luck is magic, and all magic is the devil's work. There is no such thing as luck. It is God who makes all things happen, in this life and afterwards too." I kept trying to jump up and snatch it from him, but he was still holding it too high. "It's a lucky charm, which is devil's magic, witchcraft, mumbo jumbo. You will wear a cross or nothing at all."

"Then," I said, surprised at my own sudden courage, "then I won't wear anything at all." And I turned and walked away. He strapped me that evening of course, and afterwards I had to bend my head in front of him as he put the cross around my neck. He said that if he ever saw me not wearing it, he'd strap me again. "What about my key?" I asked him.

"I've thrown it out," he said. "It's where all witchcraft belongs, in the rubbish."

That night I cried myself to sleep. Neither Wes nor Marty could comfort me. My precious key was gone, gone for ever, and I felt utterly alone in the world without it, like my last roots had been ripped out. As I lay there that night in the darkness I had murder in my heart. And I don't just mean I hated Piggy Bacon. I mean I really wanted to kill him. I might well have done it too. I had found the courage now – revenge and fury gives you powerful courage – but I just couldn't think how to do it. I had no idea how I could murder him, not yet, but I was determined to find some way to do it and do it soon. Luckily for him, luckily for me too, it didn't come to that. Luck intervened, or fate, or circumstance, call it what you like, and when it came, it came from a most welcome and unexpected source.

When I'd first come to Cooper's Station I'd been terrified of snakes, and of spiders in particular. Every day we'd see all manner of strange and wonderful creatures out on the farm, from wallabies to wombats. But it was spiders and snakes I looked out for. We'd see them everywhere, snakes curled up under the dormitory block or slithering along between the boulders down by the creek. Spiders, we discovered, loved the toilet, which was a shed with a corrugated iron roof built on to the side of the dormitory block. It was baking hot in there and stank to high heaven, but it was the spiders I hated, the spiders I feared. I feared them so much that I tried not to go to the toilet. Whenever I could I would try to go outside to do my business. Sometimes though, I was in a hurry and the toilet was nearby and I'd risk it. But I'd do it quickly, as quickly as I could, trying not to breathe in, and trying not to look for spiders.

They say you never see the bullet that gets you. It's the same with spiders. I was told later it was a redback spider. I was sitting there on the toilet. It happened when I stood up. I was pulling up my shorts and I felt it bite my foot, felt the stabbing surging pain of it, saw it scurrying away. I screamed then and ran out. I remember stumbling to my knees and Mrs Piggy running towards me.

I've no idea how long I lay in bed. Marty told me later that they all thought I was going to die. I do remember realising I wasn't in my own bed, that there were curtains and pictures on the wall, and a big cupboard. I remember too Mrs Piggy coming in and sitting with me, and I felt hot and heavy all over as if I was weighted down somehow. And once when she came she wasn't alone. She had an Aboriginal man with her, a bushman with white hair, and he looked into my eyes and felt my face and gave me a medicine to take and laid some kind of a poultice on my foot. The medicine tasted so bitter I could barely swallow it. But whatever it was that he put on my foot cooled it wonderfully.

As I got better Mrs Piggy would sit beside me playing her squeezy box and I loved that. All these memories may well not be memories at all. It was Mrs Piggy who told me afterwards when I was better, when I thanked her for looking after me, that it wasn't her that had cured me at all, but a "black fellow" she'd called in. He'd saved my life, she said, not her. "And don't say a word to Mr Bacon," she said. "He wouldn't like it. He doesn't believe in their magic. But I do. There's room for all sorts of magic and miracles in this world – that's what I think."

I'd spent the best part of a month in my sick bed in the farmhouse, so Marty told me later. He said that both Wes and he had agreed it would be almost worth a spider bite or a snake bite if it got you a month's holiday in the farmhouse. I told them everything, about how well I'd been fed and looked after, about Mrs Piggy nursing me and how kind she'd been, and all about the bushman who'd saved my life with his magical medicine. And I told them too about the last thing Mrs Piggy had done the morning I was to leave the farmhouse. She came up to my room. I was sitting on the bed buttoning my shirt.

"Here," she said. "This is yours, I think." And she handed me a tiny box, like a pill box. I opened it, and there was my key lying in a bed of cotton wool. "Hide it," she told me. "And hide it well." She said nothing more, and was gone out of the room before I could even thank her.

I never referred to her after that as Mrs Piggy, nor did anyone else because very soon everyone knew how good a person she really was, how she'd found my key, looked after it, and given it back to me. She was Ida after that, Ida to all of us. We all knew from then on that we had in her a true friend, but we didn't know just how good a friend, just how important a friend she was to be to us. We had many more gruelling months to endure before we were to find that out. And now I had my key back I forgot all about killing Piggy Bacon. So I suppose you could say Ida didn't just save my life, she saved his. Much good did it do her.

As for my key, I did as Ida had told me, I hid it well. But I kept it close too. Right above my bed there was a window, and above it a wooden lintel with a narrow split at one end, but it was just wide enough. I pushed my key in deep, so it couldn't be seen, making quite sure Piggy could never find it, and left it there. But it never left my thoughts. Every night before I got into bed I'd look up at my secret place. I told Marty – no one else.

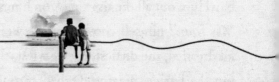

"Only One Way Out"

We could see it happening right in front of our eyes, every day, every night. And we didn't do nearly enough to prevent it. There's a lot in my life I regret, a lot to feel guilty about – too much. But I don't think anything troubles me more than what happened to Wes Snarkey at Cooper's Station. I still have dreams about it, and about him, all these years later. I should have seen it coming. I should have had the courage to stand beside him, but I didn't. Nor did

Marty, and nor did any of us, except Ida. At least Ida tried.

It all went back, I'm sure, to that glorious day when Wes knocked Piggy Bacon down in the yard, then sat on him and clobbered him. Wes became our hero that day, but he also replaced Marty as Piggy's favourite victim. He would bawl him out all the time, pick on him at every opportunity. Wes found himself chosen for the worst jobs, the ones we all dreaded, the dirtiest, the heaviest, the smelliest: cleaning out the latrine, digging ditches, carting stones. And Piggy was as clever about it as he was vicious. He knew how Wes loved to work near Big Black Jack in the stables. Everyone knew it. Wes had made no secret of his love for the horse, so Piggy deliberately saw to it that he was never anywhere near his paddock or the stable. And he made sure as well that Wes worked mainly on his own. He deliberately set out to isolate him from the rest of us.

Hardly a day went by when Wes wasn't hauled out in front of all of us at evening punishment parade. Sometimes Piggy would just bellow at him. Sometimes he would take the strap to him and give him a hiding. He'd always find some excuse, any excuse to punish him. We could all see Wes was getting it a lot harder then the rest of us. And Piggy was enjoying it too – I saw it in his face. When he whacked Wes it was always done with more venom, more violence. Thinking back, I'm ashamed to say there was even a sense in which I felt a little relieved because while Wes was on the receiving end, then at least I wasn't.

Wes grew in stature in our eyes with every whack of Piggy's belt. He never once flinched, never once complained, and so far as we knew he never even cried. For long weeks and months, it was his resistance and his defiance in the face of our hated enemy that kept us going and gave us all hope. I longed for the day that he'd have a go at Piggy again. I was sure he would. I thought, and Marty did too, that Wes was just biding his time, picking the right moment.

Then I began to notice that Wes was becoming more and more silent, more withdrawn, even with Marty and me, and we were his best friends. It happened slowly, so slowly that it was difficult at first to believe it was really happening. To start with I thought it was just because he was never allowed to be in the same working party as Marty and me, so we were simply seeing less of him. He often wasn't with us during playtime either – Piggy regularly made him work on longer than the rest of us. And even when we were together, in the dormitory, Wes seemed to be shutting himself off from us. We'd been a threesome, all pals together, but now however much Marty and I tried to include him – and we did – we could both feel him slipping away from us and turning in on himself.

In time he became almost a stranger to us, a loner, just as he'd been before during those first months at Cooper's Station. We wanted him to be one of us again because we liked him, and also because we admired him for how he was facing down the loathsome Piggy Bacon, and humiliating him every day on our behalf. I thought maybe he was dealing with it in his own way, bearing it stoically and in silence. I thought he could take it. I was wrong.

One morning Wes wouldn't get up for roll call. He lay in his bed and wouldn't move. Marty and I tried to persuade him, but he ignored us. He just turned his face away from us. We knew what would happen. Later after roll call, we were all standing out there in the cold of dawn, listening to Piggy inside the dormitory doing his worst. We heard him whacking Wes, yelling at him. "You asked for it, you little devil! I'll teach you. If it's the last thing I do, I'll teach you. No work, no food. See how you like that!" Every phrase was punctuated by the swish and whack of his stick. He was giving Wes a real pasting, and to our shame we just stood there and let it happen.

Then we heard Wes talking back, a steely calm in his voice. "I won't work for you, not ever again. And I won't eat your rotten food either. You can keep it." Moments later Piggy came storming out of the dormitory hut on to the verandah. He stood there surveying us all breathlessly, his face a beacon of rage.

For days Wes lay there refusing to get up, and every morning Piggy would go in and beat him, and every day he stopped his food too. To begin with Marty and I tried to squirrel away something for him, bread crusts perhaps. But Wes just shook his head. He wouldn't touch anything. He told us we shouldn't do it because we'd only get into trouble ourselves. And anyway, he said, there was no point, because he meant what he'd said: he wouldn't touch Piggy's food, even if it came secretly from us. He would stay on hunger strike, he said, until Piggy Bacon treated us properly and stopped beating us. He would drink water though. So we'd bring him that as often as we could. We kept bringing food too but it was no use. He'd made up his mind, he said, and nothing would change it. He would sometimes smile at us, but weakly now as if we were kind strangers.

He would say very little, and as he weakened he said less and less. But he did say something one evening when we were all three there together, Marty and I sitting on his bed. He said, and I've never forgotten his words: "You know what I think. I think there's only one way out of this place, and I've found it." Marty asked him what he meant, but he wouldn't say. We both of us tried again and again to talk him out of his hunger strike, but he was dead set on it. He wouldn't listen. I know now we should have tried harder. We should have tried much harder.

"Did We Have the Children
Here for This?"

In the end we went to the only person we thought might help. We went to the farmhouse to see Ida. We told her everything: how Wes was beaten each morning, how he was on hunger strike, how he could die if something wasn't done soon. Even while she was listening to us, she was looking around nervously. I could tell she just wanted us gone. And I could tell too that she already knew everything we'd been telling her. "You shouldn't be here," she said when we'd finished. "Go now, go quickly, before someone sees you. I'll see what I can do." And she closed the door and went back inside, leaving us standing there. I told Marty that I was sure she'd find a way to help Wes somehow.

"She'd better," he said, "or else he'll be a gonner, that's for sure."

That same night after lock-up, Ida came to the dormitory. It was the first time she'd ever come inside at night. We heard the door unlock, saw the dancing light of her torch. All of us expected it to be Piggy Bacon on one of his occasional late-night patrols so we lay doggo, feigning sleep. "I've come to see Wes," she whispered. "Which bed?"

When we heard who it was we all sat up. I took her there and showed her. She sat down on his bed and tried to talk to him. Wes didn't respond at all, not at first. He wouldn't even turn over and look at her. Everyone was there by now, gathered round his bed.

Ida put a hand on his shoulder. "I've brought you some cakes, Wes, and some milk," she said. "Please, you must eat." And she opened up the cake tin on her lap. "I've put a cherry on each one for you. You'll like them." Wes turned over then and looked up at her.

"I can't," he said. "If I eat, he'll make me work. And I won't work for him. Never again. Not ever."

She tried. For an hour or more she did all she could to tempt him, to persuade him. She told him that God helped those who helped themselves, how she understood his suffering. "And I know that God does too," she said, "because he has told me so. I prayed. I asked him what to do, and he said I must come to you and feed you. God loves us all, Wes. In our suffering, we must always remember that."

But no amount of gentle persuasion would change his mind. Even her tears didn't seem to move him. We could hear the tears in her voice as she pleaded with him, smoothing his hair all the while. Nothing she said or did made any difference. In the end she simply had to give up, just as we had before her.

We had often heard the sound of fury from the farmhouse late at night, but until now it had always been a one-sided battle, with only Piggy Bacon's voice raging and roaring, then afterwards the sound of Ida sobbing and the dog whining. This time there were two voices raised, hers as loud and as angry as his. For the first time, Ida was giving as good as she got. We could hear her every word. "The boy will die!" she cried. "Do you want that? Did we have these children here for this?" I wasn't the only one who felt like cheering her on.

"All children are sinful, born sinful," Piggy railed back, "and these are more sinful than most. My task is to cleanse them of sin, to prepare them for heaven. I won't spare the rod, because it is the only way they will learn. And the boy has to learn who is master here."

"I thought Jesus was master here," she argued. "Or did you forget that? You punish the boy only out of pride, and you know it." And so it went on. Sadly though, it ended as it so often ended, with the sound of smashing crockery, of blows, and Ida's sharp cries of pain and the dog yelping and whining. We knew Piggy was kicking him. Then silence, and sobbing.

Marty began the chorus, and raised to sudden courage we all joined in: "For she's a jolly good fellow, for she's a jolly good fellow, for she's a jolly good fellow, and so say all of us." We sang it out loud, again and again, at the top of our voices to be sure that Piggy could hear us. He heard all right. He came out of the farmhouse and bellowed at us to stop or he'd come over and whip the lot of us. So, cowed once more, we stopped. I felt even then that our silence was a betrayal. The shame of betrayal is something that never leaves you.

All of us knew that Ida had done battle for Wes and for all of us that night. None of us knew that although she may have lost the battle, she had not yet given up the fight. Wes didn't know it either, of course, which is why, I suspect, he decided to do what he did.

He disappeared the next morning, but he didn't go alone. We came back from work for our soup and bread at lunchtime as usual, and found his bed was empty. I immediately supposed that maybe Ida had come over and taken him back to the farmhouse to nurse him and look after him. So I ran over and found her at the back, digging in her vegetable garden. She hadn't seen him, she said. She left her digging and joined in the search. Everyone was looking for him now, including Piggy Bacon, who was stomping about the farm, shouting at us to look here and look there, and ranting on about how, if Wes had run off, he was going to find him and thrash the living daylights out of him. Then he discovered, or someone did, that Big Black Jack was missing too. Now he went really berserk, volcanic. I've never seen anger like it. This man of God let out a seemingly inexhaustible explosion of expletives, spat and spewed them out, all the swear words he must have been bottling up inside himself all his life.

It was quite a show, and we loved it, every moment of it. We kept our distance, of course, each of us secretly savouring the futility of his fury, celebrating his impotence. Wes had done it. He'd escaped. This was what he had been talking about to Marty and me that night on his bed, this was his "only way out". Wes had gone walkabout with Big Black Jack, and he wasn't coming back. We were all willing him to make it. I think that maybe I even prayed for it.

Piggy went after him of course. He rode out on one of the other horses, and we scanned the horizon all day hoping he wouldn't come back with Wes, but fearing the worst all the time. That evening we looked out of the windows of the dormitory hut and saw Piggy come riding in, slumped in his saddle, his face covered in dust, his lips cracked – and he was alone. He hadn't found him. Wes was still on the run. We all jumped up and down in the dormitory, clapping one another on the back, ecstatic in our triumph, not just because Wes had succeeded yet again in humbling Piggy Bacon, but also because we all of us suddenly believed that where Wes could go, we could go too. One day, somehow, we could do the same.

There was another raging row that night in the farmhouse, with Piggy calling Wes "a stinking, ungrateful little horse thief". And we heard Ida standing up to him again.

"What did you expect, treating him like you did?"

It cheered our hearts to hear her fighting back, and our response was quite spontaneous. We burst into another chorus of *For She's a Jolly Good Fellow*, and this time Piggy didn't come out to silence us. We had silenced him. Our triumph was complete, we thought. But then we heard the dingo dogs calling. We'd heard them often enough before at Cooper's Station, seen them loping about in the distance, seen one or two lying dead out in the paddock, shot by Piggy Bacon, and left there he told us as a warning to the others. We were used enough to dingoes by now. But on this night their cries struck a terrible fear in my heart. It was an omen of something, I was sure of it.

Next morning we'd had roll call and breakfast, and were just about to go out to work when we saw Big Black Jack. He was a long way off, but it was definitely him. He wasn't alone. There were a dozen or more bushmen alongside him.

With sinking hearts we looked for Wes. It wasn't until they came close that we saw him. One of the bushmen was carrying him in his arms. But Wes wasn't clinging on round his neck. His arms were hanging down. He was limp, and I knew at once he was lifeless.

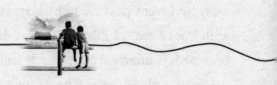

"Just Watch Me"

I've seen several dead people in my lifetime, but Wes Snarkey was the first. You don't forget the first. I thought I'd be frightened to look at him, but when it came to it, I wasn't. He was laid out on the long trestle table in the middle of our dormitory, and we stood all around in silence gazing down at him. When I first saw him I was too angry to be sad, and I was angry for all the wrong reasons. I was angry because Wes hadn't made it, angry that he'd ended our dream this way, taken away all the hope we'd vested in him. I wasn't angry at Piggy Bacon, not yet.

Someone began to whimper then, a stifled sobbing that soon spread among us all. Tears seemed to fill my entire head. One by one, unable to bear it any longer, they turned away and went outside, until Marty and I were left alone with Wes. Death, I discovered that day, is not frightening, because it is utterly still. And it is still because death, when it comes, is always over. There's only terror in it if you fear it, and ever since my first death, Wes' death, I have never feared it. It is simply the end of a story, and if you've loved the story then it is sad. And sometimes, as it was with Wes, it is an agony of sadness.

Wes did not look as if he was asleep. He did not look at peace. He was too still for that, and too pale. He was somehow smaller too, I remember that. He was cold when I touched his hand. There was a bruise on the side of his face, and cuts too. My thoughts turned then to Piggy Bacon, who we all knew had killed Wes as surely as if he had put a bullet in him. Beside me Marty echoed the hatred now burning in my heart. "Bastard!" he said, almost whispering it at first. Then he was shouting it out loud: "Bastard! Bastard!" And that was the moment we saw

Piggy Bacon standing at the door of the hut. Marty looked him straight in the eye and said it again, as good as spat it at him. "Bastard!"

Piggy seemed too stunned to hear him. He was staring down at Wes.

"Happy now?" said Marty.

This time Piggy Bacon did take in what Marty had said. I saw vengeance in his eyes, and I knew then Marty would be his next target. Ida came hurrying in then, and saw Wes lying there. For a few moments she stood there motionless, her whole face frozen. Then she walked towards the table, bent over, and kissed Wes on the forehead. She picked up his hands and arranged them, one on top of the other, and touched his bruised cheek tenderly with the back of her hand. She straightened up then, looked long and hard at Piggy Bacon, then pushed past him and went out of the door.

A doctor came, the police came. More cars up and down the farm track that day than I'd seen in all my time at Cooper's Station. They carried Wes out on a stretcher, a blanket covering him, and put him in the back of an ambulance. We stood there watching the ambulance until it disappeared in a cloud of its own dust. That was the last we ever saw of Wes Snarkey. To this day I don't know where they buried him. The bushmen stayed all that day until dusk, gathered down by the creek, crouching there unmoving, their own kind of vigil.

Ida told us later how the doctors thought Wes had died. He'd broken his neck. She thought he must have been too weak to sit on the horse through the heat of the day, that he'd probably lost consciousness and fallen off. He wouldn't have suffered, she said. It would all have been very quick. Questions were asked afterwards. Lots of official-looking people in suits and dog collars and hats came and went, in and out of the farmhouse. One or two even came over to inspect our dormitory block, and to watch us at work out on the farm. Not one of them ever talked to us. They just looked at us and made notes.

For us Wes' death changed absolutely nothing, except that we had lost our hero, and without him felt more vulnerable than ever. Piggy Bacon strutted about the place as usual, as if nothing had happened. He mentioned Wes' death only once, used it during one of his Sunday sermons. It was a favourite sermon of his, about the Ten Commandments. One Sunday he added this, to make his point: "I want you all to remember," he said, "that the last thing that boy ever did was to steal a horse, *my* horse. And look what happened to him. It was his fault, no one else's. He's only got himself to blame. 'Thou shalt not steal.' Disobey the Ten Commandments, and that's what happens to you. Let it be a lesson to you, a lesson you'll never forget."

In the days and weeks after Wes died, we saw almost nothing of Ida. She'd bring us our food, but she'd never say anything, not a word. She'd never once look at us. We never saw her out on the farm either. She didn't even appear at Piggy's side any more at Sunday services. So we had to sing our hymns unaccompanied – no squeezy box to lead us, just Piggy Bacon's trumpeting, tuneless voice. We did see her occasionally hanging out her washing on the line, and sometimes in the evening sitting alone out on the verandah of the farmhouse, her dog at her feet. But even then she seemed not to be noticing what was going on around her any more. If ever I spoke to her, she wouldn't answer me. She'd simply stare straight ahead of her as if she hadn't heard me at all. It was almost as if she was in a kind of trance. She must have been like it inside the house, too, because there were no more rows, and she played no more music on her squeezy box.

*

Ida chose a Sunday to do it. We were all standing out in the heat in front of the dormitory, Piggy up there in the shade of the verandah in his preacher's black suit, clutching his Bible. We were singing *What a friend we have in Jesus* again.

We noticed her before he did. She was telling her dog to stay where he was. He sat down, then lay down, his head on his paws. She came down the steps of the farmhouse in her apron, striding purposefully towards us – not at all how she usually walked. And she was carrying a shotgun. Suddenly no one was singing any more. Ida was standing right beside me now, and she was pointing the shotgun, levelling it at Piggy Bacon's chest.

"Children, go inside and collect your things," she said, and she said it without once taking her eyes off Piggy Bacon's face. "Quickly now, children. Quickly now." We were rooted to the spot. Not one of us moved. But Piggy did. He made to come towards her, to step down off the verandah. Ida's voice was ice-cold. "Don't think I won't use this if I have to," she said. And then to us, "Hurry children. Bring everything you need. You won't be coming back."

"Have you gone mad, Ida?" Piggy was trying to bellow at her, but it came out more like a squeal of fury. "What are you doing?"

"I'm setting them free," she told him, "that's what I'm doing. And it's true, I *have* been mad. All this, this building we put up, this orphanage, everything we've done, and done in the name of the Lord, too, has been a great madness. But I'm not mad any more. You don't show God's love to little children by hurting them, by working them till they drop, and certainly not by killing them. It's over. I'm letting them go."

We didn't wait any more. We rushed up the steps past Piggy Bacon and into the dormitory. Jubilant at the completely unexpected turn of events, we threw all the clothes and belongings we had into our suitcases, and ran out again, eager not to miss the drama unfolding out there. I was leaping off the verandah steps, suitcase in hand, when I remembered my lucky key. There was no way I was going to leave it behind. I rushed back in again and climbed up on to my bed. I could just spot it deep inside the crack in the lintel, but I couldn't get at it to hook it out – my nails just weren't long enough. I don't think I could have managed to retrieve it at all if Marty hadn't come back to find me. He lent me his penknife and out it came, easily. I had my lucky key.

Back outside, Piggy Bacon was standing there, hovering between bewilderment and fury. Ida still had the shotgun aimed at him, her finger on the trigger. "Now children," she said, "I want you all to stand way back, right back. Go on now." We did as she told us. When I looked at her again she was holding the shotgun on Piggy with one hand, and with the other was taking something out of the pocket of her apron – it looked to me like a wet rag, nothing more. Piggy seemed to realise at once what she was doing, long before we did. He kept begging and begging her not to do it, but by now she was walking up the steps of the dormitory, sideways, keeping the gun pointing at him all the time.

"Stay where you are," she warned him.

"Don't do it, Ida," he cried. "Please, you can't."

"Just watch me," she replied coolly. That was when I caught a whiff of it. Diesel oil. And suddenly we all knew what she was going to do. "I'm going to burn this place to the ground," she said, "so there'll be nowhere for them to stay. Then you'll have to let them go, won't you?" And with that she disappeared into the dormitory. We saw her moments later through the window, lighting the rag with a match, saw the curtains catch fire. Then she was coming out, and there was smoke billowing out of the door behind her. She came down the steps and threw the shotgun down at Piggy's feet.

"There," she said. "It's done."

"For She's a Jolly Good Fellow"

There was a frozen moment before Piggy Bacon moved. Then he bent and snatched up the shotgun. "It's not loaded," Ida said quietly. Piggy broke open the gun and looked. I've never ever seen a man snarl like Piggy did then. You could see the beast in his eyes as he charged up the steps into the dormitory. He tried first to beat the flames out with a blanket. We could hear him choking and spluttering inside. There was more smoke now, but already fewer flames. My heart sank. The curtains were on fire, but nothing else seemed to have caught. Piggy Bacon yanked off the curtains, cursing loudly.

Moments later he came rushing out, and ran to the line of wash buckets on the verandah. At this point Ida tried to stop him, but he pushed her aside angrily and sent her sprawling. With a bucket in each hand, the water spilling out over, he disappeared inside again. There were no more flames to be seen after that. The next time we saw him he came staggering out bent double and coughing his lungs out. But when he stood up he was smiling. Ida was lying there crying on the verandah, sobbing as if her heart would break.

Suddenly Marty began singing, quite softly at first, but very deliberately: *For She's a Jolly Good Fellow.* Soon we were all singing, and singing it out loud. It had become in that moment our song of defiance. We sang it right at him to show him just what we thought of him, and just as much we sang it for Ida to make her feel better, to thank her for what she'd tried to do for us, to show solidarity. Piggy screamed at us to stop, but we didn't. We kept on and on, all of us fired with new courage, and new fury too. Then I did perhaps the bravest thing I ever did in all my life, before or since, I went up those steps and helped Ida to her feet. I got the strap for it, ten strokes, but then we all got the strap that day. Marty got fifteen, because Piggy said he was the ringleader.

That night in the dormitory was the worst I can remember. The whole hut still reeked of smoke, a constant reminder to us of how Ida had so nearly succeeded in her brave attempt to set us free. We felt completely deflated and defeated. Hopes had been lifted so high that the disappointment, when it came as suddenly as it had, was all the more cruel. I cried into my pillow. Outside the cry of the dingoes echoed my sadness. Very few of us didn't cry ourselves to sleep that night.

It was still night-time when I was woken. Marty was shaking me awake, his hand over my mouth. "Get up," he whispered. "Get up. Get dressed. We're getting out of here."

I was still half-asleep, still half-dressed, trying to gather my thoughts. "But the door's locked," I said. "Piggy always locks the door, you know he does." Marty shushed me, took me by the arm and we tiptoed towards the door of the hut, carrying our boots.

Only one of the others stirred as we passed, he just sat up, and looked blankly at us. "You woke me," he moaned. Then he lay down, and went straight back to sleep again.

Marty turned the handle, and miraculously the door opened. Marty took great care as he shut it behind us. We crept out on to the verandah, sat on the top step and put our boots on. He answered my question before I could ask it. "Ida did it," he whispered. "I told her we were going to make a break for it tonight, but we needed the door unlocked. I thought she'd do it, but I wasn't sure. But she did, didn't she? Come on."

We ran then, but not out into the bush as I'd thought we would. Instead, Marty was leading me in the direction of the farmhouse. I was wondering what he was up to, where he was going, when I realised we weren't heading for the farmhouse at all, but rather for the stables. Big Black Jack jumped a bit in his skin when he first saw us. But he seemed happy enough when Marty put his halter on him and led him out. Ida's dog barked then from the farmhouse, which sent shivers up the back of my neck. "Shut up, dog," Marty hissed, and shut up he did, just like that. I knew then that Ida had done that for us too.

We climbed up on to the back of one of the farm carts and mounted Jack from there – he was a big horse, it was the only way up for us. Marty rode in front, me behind, hanging on. Then we just walked him away into the night. We didn't go up the farm track, because we knew that way must lead to a settlement or a town of some kind, and we wanted to keep well clear of people. If anyone saw us, they'd be bound to take us back. So we deliberately went the other way, down a gully and out into the bush. We didn't look back. I didn't ever want to set eyes on that place ever again. But I did say a silent goodbye to those we were leaving behind in the dormitory, and to Ida who had risked so much to give us our freedom.

Neither Marty nor I spoke, not for a long time, not until we'd put at least half an hour between ourselves and Piggy Bacon. By then we were trotting, and we couldn't talk because we were laughing so much. We had done it; we had escaped! And Big Black Jack was huffing and puffing underneath us, laughing along with us, I thought, revelling in his new-found freedom every bit as much as we were. But after a while I got to thinking about all the others we'd left behind at Cooper's Station, that maybe we should have taken them all with us. (All these years later I still feel bad about that. Why is it you never forget what you feel bad about?)

Marty started singing *London Bridge is Falling Down* then, softly at first, then I joined in, and soon we were bellowing it out over the bush.

I kept asking Marty questions, the most important first. "Where are we going? Which direction?"

"Away," he said. "Anywhere just so long as it's away."

"You been planning this? You never said anything."

"That's because I didn't think of it until punishment parade yesterday evening," he said. "It was while he was hitting me. I knew I'd be next, that he'd go after me just like he did with Wes. If I'd stayed he'd have killed me. Sooner or later, he'd have killed me. I know he would. Then I just got lucky. I saw Ida by the stables just before lock-up, told her what I needed. She didn't even have to think about it. She did say one thing though: I had to remind you about your lucky key, to be sure you took it with you. Hope you have, because I'm not going back, not for all the tea in China."

My heart was in my mouth. I hadn't given it a second thought. But I felt in my pocket, and there it still was. "Got it," I told him.

"That's good," Marty said, "because we're going to need it. We're going to need all the luck we can get."

It was fear of getting caught, and sheer exhilaration that we were free, that kept us going that night. We knew that we mustn't stop, not for a moment, or even slow down, because Piggy would be sure to be coming after us just as soon as he discovered we were missing, and that would be at roll call at dawn. We had until then to get as far away as possible. Big Black Jack didn't want to trot for long, but he plodded on steadily, never tiring, and we sat up there the two of us, rocking our way towards the grey light of dawn. We were just so happy to be out of Cooper's Station. We talked a lot as we rode, and we laughed, laughed as hard as we could. I remember I felt cocooned by the night, swallowed up in its immensity, protected. At one point we saw some lights on the horizon. It looked like a settlement of some kind, so we kept our distance. We sang to the stars, all the millions of them up there. We sang *For She's a Jolly Good Fellow* till we were hoarse with it. They seemed so close those stars, close enough to hear us.

It was cold, very cold that night. We had no water. We had no food. But none of that worried us. Not yet. We were too happy to be worried. Not even the cry of the dingoes bothered us. Only when the sun came up, and the bush came alive all about us, only then did we begin to feel alone in this wild and unfamiliar place with nothing but scrub and trees for miles around in every direction. We'd been following a dried-up creek for a while when I felt the first heat of the sun. That was when I first thought I wanted to drink. We had stopped talking to one another now. There was no more laughter. I was beginning to realise just how vast this place was and just how lost we were. I didn't like to say it though. Big Black Jack was walking on, purposeful and surefooted as ever. He seemed to know where he was going, and that made me feel better.

When finally Marty did say something though, it just confirmed my own worst fears. "I don't like this," he said. "We've been here before, when it was darker. We were coming the other way then. And I keep thinking something else too, something Wes told me once, and Wes knew all about horses. He said that a horse will never get itself lost. It'll always know the way home. I think maybe Big Black Jack is taking us back, back to Cooper's Station."

Wide as the Ocean

How easily we fell into despair, the two of us. As we left the shade of the gum trees how quickly the heat of the sun sapped our strength, and our spirits too. The desire for water was fast becoming a craving. The need to find it became obsessive. Within just a few hours all we could talk about, however hard we tried not to, was water. I didn't care any longer if Big Black Jack was walking straight back to Cooper's Station, right up to the farmhouse, nor if Piggy

Bacon might be tracking us down and coming after us. Every shimmering watery horizon we saw raised our hopes, but we soon found we could not trust even the evidence of our eyes. Mirages mocked us time and again. We tried our best to ignore them. But a mirage is only a mirage once you've discovered it's a mirage. Until then it's a pool of cold clear water just waiting for you, a pool of hope. More than once this cruel hoax set Marty and me arguing with one another. But in the end we didn't even have the energy for that.

The deep gully we were following was sandy, but up on the banks there were patches of brambles and scrub, and here and there clusters of stringy bark gum trees. Where there were trees, we thought there must be water. Little did we know. So we rode down the dried up gully, hoping all the while to discover a hidden pool in the shadows, but everywhere we found nothing but earth turned to dust. There wasn't a sign of moisture. And all through this futile search the sun rose ever higher, blazed hotter.

Gathering enough thoughts to decide anything was so difficult. But we did manage to concentrate enough to make one decision between us. We invested in it all our last hopes. We could see the ground ahead of us on one side of the gully rising steeply into a granite cliff. From the top of this cliff we thought we must be able to see for miles around, that from up there we'd be bound to spot a river perhaps or a pool. But Big Black Jack refused to be diverted from the gully, and we knew already he was far too strong to argue with. He went where he wanted to go and that was all there was to it. So in the end we had to get off him and lead him up the slope to the highest point of the cliff.

The whole of Australia lay before us, it seemed, as wide as the ocean, and just as inhospitable too. We could see the gully winding its way through the bush, other gullies joining it to make one great swathe of sand through the scrub, but there was no glint of water anywhere, not a shimmer to be seen. Now I really was beginning to hope that Piggy Bacon would find us, and take us back to Cooper's Station. I didn't care about the beating I knew he'd give us. I thought only of the wash buckets on the verandah, of plunging my head in and then drinking all of them dry one by one.

Marty was not lost in reverie as I was. He had not given up so easily. He was pointing excitedly at what he swore must be a place where there was water, and certainly in the distance there seemed to be a patch of much greener, lusher vegetation around some very tall trees. It was miles away and did not look at all promising to me. I didn't say so though. "If it's green, then there's got to be water somewhere," Marty said. "Got to be. Come on." Even if there had been a convenient rock from which to mount, I don't think either of us would have had the strength to do it. We could only manage to walk now with the greatest effort. So we led Big Black Jack down the hill and into the gully again.

We found Marty's promised oasis, but doing it drained us utterly of the last of our will power. There were trees, and it was green, but we could find no water. By now the sun had worked its worst on us. My head was swimming so much I often thought I would faint. I kept stumbling, and so did Marty. Breathing heavily now and lathered up, Big Black Jack wandered away from us into the deepest shade, put his head against the trunk of a tree and rested on three legs. Like us, he'd had enough. He could do no more. He was telling us in his own way that we should do it too, that we should never have ventured out in the heat of the day in the first place.

We lay down nearby. I curled up against Marty's back for comfort. "We'll be all right," he said to me, but I knew how far we were from all right. Even so it cheered me a little to hear him say it. I tried not to think that if I slept I might never wake up again, but I thought it all the same. Sleep, when it came, was so welcome.

It was evening when I woke and I knew at once we were not alone. They were crouching a few paces away, a dozen of them perhaps, bushmen, men and boys. They were studying us intently, as still as the rocks around them. I shook Marty until he sat up and took notice. "It's the same ones," he whispered, "the same ones that brought Wes back. I recognise them."

"Say something," I said. "You've got to say something."

"Drink," Marty mimed it as he spoke. "Water. We need water. Understand?" That was when the tallest of them came forward and crouched down close to us. I recognised him then. It was the old bushman who had come to Ida's house that day and treated my spider bite. He smiled at me like a stranger you've met before who is happy you've remembered him. He held out his cupped hands. His hands were full of fruit, red fruit, green fruit, like plums but rounder. We ate them. We drank them. We devoured them. I don't remember the taste, but I remember savouring the juice of each one, sucking out every drop of it. They gave Big Black Jack some too, which he snuffled up eagerly.

Then they motioned to us to stand up, to mount up. We tried, but they soon saw we couldn't do it without their help. I was lifted up effortlessly and sat astride Big Black Jack. So was Marty, who was sitting behind me now and hanging on. One of the bushmen took the reins, and led us along the gully. They were all around us, the children among them smiling up at us now. When I smiled back they laughed out loud, and I knew they were not laughing at me, but out of sheer delight. It touches me even now when I think of it. It was a little moment, and at the same time a great moment, one I have treasured always.

"They're taking us back," Marty whispered in my ear, "like they did with Wes."

"Only we're not dead," I said.

Within an hour or so they brought us through some scrubby trees to a hidden pool, a basin of dark rock. A cool evening breeze rippled the surface of the water. We needed no invitation and nor did Big Black Jack. He trotted to the edge and was drinking even before we managed to tumble off him. We were alongside him then, all three of us, one muzzle and two mouths drinking in all we could. Then Big Black Jack was shaking his dribbles all over us, and the bushmen were laughing. They drank too, but they were in no hurry. They did not gulp greedily as we had. Instead they scooped it up one-handed and sipped. In no time a fire was going. They speared some fish and cooked them. I tried to eat slowly as they did, but it wasn't easy. And there was more fruit afterwards, more berries. Big Black Jack browsed nearby. We could hear his jaws grinding, his teeth crunching. He was eating well too.

I expected we would sleep then because night was coming on fast, but we didn't. Instead they lifted us up again on to Big Black Jack, and together we moved on into the gathering dark. When I looked up I found that the stars were up there again filling the sky from end to end. I thought then of the night before, of how happy we'd been to be free, how we'd sung to the stars. And now we were being taken back to Cooper's Station, and there was nothing whatsoever we could do about it. I wondered why the bushmen were doing it, whether Piggy was paying them for hunting us down and bringing us back. But I thought that couldn't be right, that after all these were the people I'd seen him driving away from the farm with his horse whip when they strayed too close. I did whisper to Marty that we could try to tell them we didn't want to go back, but he thought it was pointless.

"They wouldn't understand a word we said," he told me. "So what's the point?"

All night long I dreaded the morning and the first sight of Cooper's Station, dreaded the thought of standing there on punishment parade, hand outstretched, trying to hold back the tears. The more I thought about it, the more I feared the coming of morning. That was why I took my lucky key out of my pocket and clutched it tight, so tight that it hurt me. I wanted to squeeze the luck out of it, to have all of it now because I needed it now more than ever before in my life.

But I began to worry that maybe even my lucky key would not be enough. So I prayed as well. I thought of Ida, then of all she had done for us, of the trouble she'd be in if Piggy found out she'd unlocked the door for us. I felt for the little wooden cross I wore around my neck. I touched it, remembering her. And then holding it I prayed for her. But if I'm honest, I think I prayed mostly for myself. Whether it was the key or the cross that did it I shall never know. I've been trying to work that one out ever since. I still am.

"Couple of Raggedy Little Scarecrows"

It wasn't until a few more days had passed that Marty and I could begin to hope that the bushmen weren't taking us back to Cooper's Station after all. Neither of us could believe these people were lost. They seemed to know every root, every tree, every gully in this maze of a wilderness. The fruit they found was never a surprise, nor the roots they dug up, nor the pools they led us to. They knew exactly where they were. They belonged in this place.

They found their way through the bush with such obvious ease that it was quite impossible to think they could ever get lost here. So if they were not lost, and we were not being deliberately led around in circles, and if after all this time we had still not yet reached Cooper's Station, then it stood to reason we weren't going there. So where were they taking us then? Marty and I asked each other that question more than a few times. But we had no answers.

With every hour that passed, the bush around us looked less and less familiar. We were in much greener country. There were hills about us, and more farms and settlements in the valleys – which the bushmen seemed to want to avoid as much as we did. We knew now, for whatever reason, that they were not taking us back. And the longer we were with them the more sure we became that these people were absolutely no threat to us. They might not talk to us. They might keep their distance. They might still stare at us more than we liked, but there was never the slightest hint of hostility towards us. On the contrary they seemed very protective of us, and as fascinated by us as we were by them. And the children found us endlessly funny, particularly when we smiled, so we smiled a lot. But then we felt like smiling. They shared their food with us: berries, roots, fruit and baked wallaby once. We had all the water we needed.

Marty did try once or twice to ask where we were going, but was simply given more fruit or berries as an answer. So he gave up. But up on Big Black Jack, as we rode through the night, or resting in the shade, the two of us speculated at length. Maybe we weren't being taken anywhere. I mean, they never looked as if they were going anywhere in particular. They just looked as if they were quite happy simply going, simply being. Or maybe they were adopting us into their tribe and we'd wander the bush with them for the rest of our lives. Maybe they were still making up their minds what to do with us. Perhaps we'd just wake up one day and find them gone. We really didn't mind. All we could be sure of was that we were a long, long way from Cooper's Station now, and further every day. Where we were going wasn't important. Sometimes at night we'd see lights in the distance, more settlements probably, but we never once thought of running off. We were safe with them. We had no reason to leave them.

I can't say exactly how many days and nights our journey lasted – it could have been five or six days perhaps. I do know that it lasted long enough for Marty and I to begin to believe it might be permanent, that we had indeed been adopted in some way. I certainly was beginning to feel comfortable among them, not because they became any less reserved – they didn't. Distance seemed to be important to them. The children though were a different story. We very soon got beyond just smiling and laughing. We splashed each other in the pools. We skimmed stones, threw sticks, ambushed one another. One took to riding piggyback on Marty's back, and the smallest of them would often ride up with us on Big Black Jack loving every moment of it. We were finding our place among them, beginning to feel accepted. That's why, when our journey finally ended, we felt all the more abandoned, even rejected.

We had been travelling through hilly country for a day or two now, and Big Black Jack was finding it very hard going, and not just because of the hills either. We knew already that kangaroos made him nervous, but there hadn't been many of them until now. Now they were everywhere, and he was not happy. In the half-dark we could see their shifting shapes, and so could Big Black Jack. We could feel him tensing beneath us. We'd talk to him to try to calm him, smooth his neck, pat him gently, but nothing seemed to work. His ears would be twitching frantically. He'd toss his head and snort at them. Worst of all, he'd just stop without any warning. Falling off was all too easy. It amused the children hugely, but was painful for us. In the end Marty and I decided it would be better altogether, and safer too, to give Big Black Jack a rest, and walk. So during the last couple of nights of our journey we walked with the bushmen, one of us leading Big Black Jack. He seemed happier that way. He puffed less and snorted less. The last night we were with them I felt as if I really was one of them, sharing the silence and the stars.

The next morning at sun-up we were coming to the top of a high hill. It had been a long steep climb. Below us was a wide green valley with a stream running through, and trees, more trees than I'd ever seen in my life. In front of us on the crest of the hill the bushmen had stopped and were talking among themselves. I thought we'd be resting here for a while, and was only too happy about that because my legs were tired, and I was longing for food and for sleep. I sat down to investigate a thorn in my foot which had been troubling me. Beside me Big Black Jack was cropping the grass contentedly.

Suddenly Marty called out. "They're going! They're leaving us!" Sure enough, the bushmen were walking away from us back the way we'd come, the children looking over their shoulders at us from time to time as they went. We called after them again and again, but they didn't stop. Then they rounded the side of the hill and were gone.

"Why?" Marty said. "Why here? Why did they leave us here?"

We stood there in silence, each of us trying to make some sense of what was happening to us, of why they had treated us this way. We felt utterly bewildered. The parting had been so unexpected, so sudden and strange. No goodbyes, not even the wave of a hand.

That was when Big Black Jack began snorting again. I looked around for kangaroos. There were none, not that I could see anyway. But Big Black Jack had stopped eating in mid-chew. He had his head up now and his ears pricked. He whinnied loud and long, so that the valley rang with it. He was lifting his nose, sniffing the air, and listening. We could hear kookaburras and galahs, all the cackle of the bush at daybreak, but certainly nothing out of the ordinary. But then we heard the sound of whistling, of someone singing, a woman singing, and with it the tread of a horse in among the trees below us, of a saddle creaking. Big Black Jack whinnied again.

A great bay horse was coming out of the trees and up the hills towards us, on its back a rider in a wide-brimmed straw hat. But it wasn't the horse or the rider that we were looking at so much as the cavalcade that was following along behind, a cavalcade of creatures, all of them infants: wombats, wallabies, joeys. And as the rider came closer I could see there was a koala clinging on round her neck, looking at me over her shoulder. She rode right up to us, let the horses touch noses and check each other over. Meanwhile she took off her hat and looked us up and down. I haven't forgotten the first words she spoke to us:

"Strewth," she said. "Look what the cat brought in. But maybe it wasn't the cat, right? How'd you get here?"

"It was the bushmen," Marty told her.

"I thought as much. Are you waifs and strays then? They only bring me waifs and strays. They know I collect them, see. They don't eat the little ones, not unless they've got to. Good people they are. Just about the best, I'd say. Where are you from?"

"England," I said. There was a wombat rooting around my feet now.

"S'all right. He won't bite," she told me. "You've come fair ways then."

"We were at Cooper's Station," Marty said. "We escaped."

"I know Cooper's Station. Mr Bacon's place, right? Where's he's got all those orphan kids." She looked us up and down.

"He used to be the preacher in town before they moved out there," she continued. "If there's one thing I can't abide it's fanatics of any kind, and religious ones are the worst of all. Running away from that place seems a pretty sensible thing to do. You'll be looking for somewhere to stay then."

Marty and I looked at one another. She was turning her horse now and walking away from us, her little animals following her. "Well, are you coming or aren't you?" she called out. "If you are, then bring the poor old black horse with you. He needs feeding up by the looks of him. Come to that, so do you. Couple of raggedy little scarecrows, that's what you are. I'll soon fatten you up. Come along if you're coming. Don't spend too long thinking about it. Haven't got all day."

Marty and I didn't need to think twice about it. We followed along behind the cavalcade, and like us Big Black Jack had a new spring in his step. "That lucky key of yours," said Marty. "You still got it?"

"Yes," I replied.

"Just don't ever lose it, that's all," he said.

Henry's Horrible Hat Hole

Big Black Jack knew it too, just as we did. We all knew we were coming home. He stepped out with new heart, snorting in his excitement all the while at the procession of creatures in front of him. Clearly size mattered to Big Black Jack when it came to kangaroos – the little joey hopping alongside the lady on the horse wasn't a worry to him at all. Nothing worried him now, nothing worried any of us. If we had been in hell at Cooper's Station before, now we were riding into paradise.

We were looking all the while for a house of some kind. But all we could see were trees and green paddocks, and beyond them the winding river, and in the distance the bluest mountains I ever saw. Suddenly there it was, a long low shack of a place, a chimney at one end and a verandah all around. There was a pond nearby which cackled with geese that came out to greet us as we arrived, followed by a flurry of hens and chicks. This was to turn out to be our home for the next seven years, the first real home I ever had, the home of my childhood. And I've been grateful all my life ever since, to Ida and to those bushmen who brought us there, who must have sensed all along what we needed.

She called it the Ark, and it didn't take much to see why. The place was alive with every conceivable domestic animal: goats, sheep, a couple of pigs, a mournful-looking donkey called Barnaby, three milk cows and their calves, and of course, her entire family of wild creatures. The domestic animals all had names, but I only remember Barnaby and a cow called Poogly – not a name you easily forget.

She didn't give names to the wild ones, she said, because they were just passing through, except for one. Henry was a wombat. Henry, she said, was probably still asleep, and didn't much like strangers. He'd been with her for seven years. He'd come and just stayed. He lived in a hole under the verandah steps, and collected hats. In fact he stole hats, any hat he could find, which was why she kept her hat on all the time. Henry slept on his hoard of hats down there in his hole and was very happy, probably the happiest wombat in the entire world, she said, which wasn't difficult, she added, because wombats generally are not the happiest of creatures.

"You can have a look later for yourself," she told us, "just don't breathe in while you're doing it. It's horrible down there. Stinks to high heaven. Not a great one for personal hygiene, our Henry."

She introduced her entire menagerie of animals before she even introduced herself. She did that over a glorious breakfast of eggs, and toast and jam, and milk, which we wolfed down, still unable to take in our extraordinary turn of luck. She waited until every last crumb was gone, every last drop. We discovered soon that this was always the thing with her. She could sense intuitively the needs and fears of us all, of all her "children", which is why, from the very first day, we always felt so at ease with her, why we came to love and trust her as we did, whether we were boys or joeys. She'd saved all of us. We didn't love her because we owed her, but because of the kind of person she was.

She wanted to hear our story. So Marty told her everything – he was always better at words than me. I watched her as she listened, saw the sadness and anger in her face. I could see she was older under her hat than I'd first imagined. When you're young you can't work out the age of an adult – they're just quite old, old, or very old. She was old, and (I'm guessing now because I never asked her of course) about fifty-five. Her hair was long to the shoulders, and grey, going to white around her temples, and this belied the youth in her face. She was quick to smile, and when she did her whole being seemed to light up. She laughed easily too. I've forgotten so much about her, so much about everything, but I can hear her laugh still. It warmed me then. It warms me now when I think of it, because there was love in her laughter, never mockery, unless it was self-mockery. And there was a directness about the way she looked at you, and the way she spoke to you.

"Well, you've told me your little tale," she began, "so I'll tell you mine. Then we'll know one another better, won't we?"

And so she told us who she was and what she was doing living there in the Ark with all her creatures around her, and Henry down his hat hole. We listened agog, because she was a wonderful storyteller. She could paint pictures in your head with words, and she could touch the heart of you too.

"Megs Molloy, that's me – Margaret really – but Aunty Megs will be fine. Just call me that, everyone does. I do a little of everything, a bit of farming, write a bit of poetry – love that – and I make boats too in my shed, because Mick made boats. You'll see photos of him about the place. He was my husband, but I lost him in the war, which was sad for me, but sadder still for him. His ship was sunk in some convoy, so he's part of the seabed now. It's as good a place to end up as any, I reckon. He made model boats all his life, sailed them too, all kinds, a destroyer in the end. Boats were his life, boats and me. So now I make boats because he taught me how to do it, and I love it. But I don't get all maudlin about Mick, not often anyway. Life's too short.

"Besides there's too much needs doing round here. Years ago when Mick and me first came here, he discovered a dead wallaby up on the road – knocked down and killed by some stupid truck. He saw a little head sticking out of her pouch, and alive, alive o! So he brought it home. That was near enough twenty years ago now. That little fellow was the first of hundreds, thousands now maybe. From that day on one of us would check the road every morning at dawn, and whenever we found an orphan, a possum, a joey, a wombat, we'd bring him home. And in time the bushmen must have got to hear about it, because they would bring along little fellows they'd found and leave them with us. They don't say much, but they've got their hearts in the right place.

"But we wouldn't ever keep them. We wouldn't cuddle them either. None of that. We'd just feed the little fellows and look after them. Tried never to tame them, never even touch them 'less we had to. Once you tame them they'll never go back to the wild. So we just kept them till they were strong enough. Then we'd all take a hike together up into the hills, and if one or two stayed up there, that was fine with us, that was just what we wanted. They were back where they belonged.

"When the war came along and Mick joined the navy, I went on doing it just the same. And when he didn't come back, I carried on. Seemed the right thing to do. So here I am writing my poetry, making my boats, looking after whoever or whatever I find out there that needs me. Then this morning, I find something I've never found before – a couple of raggedy little scarecrows left behind for me by the bushmen. So I said to myself: *they've done that for a good reason*. And now I know the reason. So I know why you were there, and now you know why I was there. Just like all the little fellows out there, you can stay as long as you need to."

The two of us walked out afterwards to see Big Black Jack in his paddock. He was trying to make friends with Aunty Megs' horse and with Barnaby. But Barnaby wasn't having any of it, and he didn't much like it either when Jack started checking out Aunty Megs' horse. I could hear Aunty Megs singing from inside the house and I felt I was the luckiest person alive. I didn't pinch myself, but I wondered more than once that first day whether Marty and I were living inside some wonderful shared dream, that maybe we'd wake up and be back at Cooper's Station again.

But when I woke up the next morning, I woke up to see Marty still fast asleep in the bed opposite, and high on a shelf all around the room models of sailing boats, and I knew the dream was not a dream at all. I heard a shuffling under my bed then, peered underneath and saw a wombat looking back up at me. He had one of my socks in his mouth. Aunty Megs was at the door then with a glass of milk for each of us. "I see you've met Henry then," she said. "Forgot to tell you. He steals socks too."

I Must Go Down to the Sea

It turned out that Henry didn't just pinch hats and socks, he'd steal just about anything that he fancied. So we never left our clothes lying around, nor shoes, nor towels. Aunty Megs told us to shoo him out of the house whenever he came in; but somehow, sooner or later, he'd always find a way back in again. And Aunty Megs was right, he did smell. If he was in the house we'd smell him before we saw him, and the stink of him lingered long in the air after we'd put him out. But we loved him all the same, just as Aunty Megs did. I think it was because of the way he looked up at you. His eyes said: "OK, so I stink. OK, so I'm a thief. But nobody's perfect, are they? So give me a break, will you? Deep down you know you love me, everyone does."

Feeding Henry his bottle of milk was the chore that was never a chore. Marty and I would often squabble over which of us should do this last task of the day. Whoever won would sit on the verandah steps right above Henry's hole. He'd climb up on to your lap, roll over on his back and wait for it. Aunty Megs said he'd just never grown up, that she'd tried and tried to break him of the habit, but he'd hang around her feet making her feel so guilty that she couldn't resist him. So Henry still got his milk, and it had to be out of a bottle.

We did have tasks at the Ark. We milked the cows, and the goats – learned to make butter and cheese too. We chopped wood, we fed the hens, got chased by the geese when we tried to shut them up in case the dingoes came in the night. But now it was work we wanted to do, because we wanted to help out, and because both of us loved being with Aunty Megs. Our hands blistered, our backs ached, but we didn't mind. Every morning she'd take us down to the main road a mile or so away, and we'd walk along the verges, one of us on the right, one of us on the left, looking for any casualties. Most days we'd find something but more often than not they'd be dead already. But from time to time we'd get lucky.

I remember the first time I discovered a joey crouched trembling by the side of his dead mother. I couldn't contain my excitement, and yelled for Aunty Megs, who came running over to pick him up. She was very strict about handling them. She never allowed us to feed them or handle them. If they were very small she'd keep them for a while in a box by the stove in the kitchen. We could crouch over them and look, but not touch. But as soon as they were old enough they'd live outside in the compound with the others. Marty and I would spend hours out there watching through the wire, but Aunty Megs was the only one allowed in. And she never talked to them, never stroked them. She just fed them.

She'd never let us come with her either when she went off for her rides into the bush, the orphan animals, her "little fellows", trailing behind her. If we came, she said, we'd only confuse them. There was no point in saving them at all, she insisted, unless they could be returned back into the wild again successfully. She made it perfectly clear that this wasn't an exercise in sentimentality, wasn't just to make herself feel good. It was to give them a second chance of life, a chance they all deserved. It was a chance everyone deserved, she said, animals and people alike.

Aunty Megs had a station wagon she kept in the farm shed, which was half hen-house and half garage. And because the hens liked sitting on the station wagon it was just about the messiest car I've ever seen in my life. But we loved it. Going into town, ten or so miles away, was a real treat. She often sang when she was driving. She used to sing a lot – it made her feel happy, she said. She'd teach us all her songs, and we'd sing along, all three of us making a dreadful racket, but we loved it. She knew all the words and all the verses of *London Bridge is Falling Down*, which was more than I did before I met her.

We didn't go into town often, just once a week or so. She'd stride down the street in her straw hat, and we'd follow along behind. Everyone knew her and she knew everyone. They were all rather curious about us at first. She didn't explain who we were or where we'd come from. She just said we were her "boys" and that was that. And it was true. We were her children, and she was our mother – the only mother we'd ever known anyway.

It was on the first of those trips into town that she took us into the police station. She'd been thinking, she told us on the drive in, and it was time someone did something about it. She wouldn't say anything else. She led us up to the desk and said we had to tell the sergeant right there and then all about Cooper's Station, everything we'd told her. So we did. The policeman wrote it all down and shook his head a lot while doing it. Aunty Megs told us sometime later that the place had been closed down, that all the children had been found other homes to go to. I was pleased about that, cockahoop that Piggy wouldn't be beating any more children. But most of all I was very sad for Ida. I remember feeling that I really didn't want to know anything to do with that place, I wanted to forget all about it. Just the name, Cooper's Station, was enough to make me think about it, and I didn't want to have to think about it ever again.

But what you *want* to think about isn't necessarily what you *do* think about. The truth is that the memories of all that happened at Cooper's Station have come back to haunt me all my life, even during those happy, happy years we spent with Aunty Megs. They were happy because I was as close then as I've ever been to carefree. I know when I read what I've just written that it sounds as if I'm wallowing in nostalgia, making an idyll of the Ark. It's difficult not to. After Cooper's Station anything would have seemed like heaven on earth.

Aunty Megs may have been the kindest person in the world, but she could be firm – we soon discovered that. She was appalled when it became clear – as of course it very soon did – that neither Marty nor I had been to school, and so neither of us could read properly nor write. So from then on she'd sit us down every morning at the kitchen table and teach us, regular as clockwork. I won't pretend that either of us were willing pupils – we just wanted to be outside messing around, climbing trees, riding Big Black Jack, making camps, talking to Henry or Poogly or trying to cheer up poor old Barnaby. It took hours sometimes to get an *ee-aw* out of Barnaby. An *ee-aw* we reckoned was as good as a laugh, so we always stayed with him till we got one. And when it rained we'd far prefer to be out with Aunty Megs in her big garden shed where she made her model boats, where we'd make them with her – she taught us that too.

But lessons, she said, had to come first. We didn't argue

with her, not because we were ever even remotely frightened of her, but because both of us knew that she always had our best interests at heart. She made no secret of her affection for us, nor her wish to give us the best upbringing she could. "One day," she told us, "you'll have to leave here and go out into the big world out there and earn your living like everyone else. To do that you need to learn. The more you learn now, the more interesting your life will be." So the two of us buckled down to our lessons, often reluctantly perhaps, but without protest.

As part of her teaching Aunty Megs told us stories, tales she'd learned from the bushmen, folk tales from England. She'd read us legends. By the stove in the evenings she'd read us a novel, a chapter a night, *Treasure Island* by Robert Louis Stevenson (we asked for that again and again). There were the *Just So Stories* by Rudyard Kipling, *Little House on the Prairie* and *Heidi*. She loved *Heidi*, and she was going to read it to us, she said, even though she knew it was a girl's book. But our favourites were the *William* books by Richmal Crompton. Sometimes she'd be laughing so much she couldn't go on. (Later when we could read properly, we read a bit of one of them to Barnaby, but he didn't find it funny at all. Not a single *ee-aw*.)

But most of all Aunty Megs loved poetry. It was Mick, she said, who had given her a love for the sound of words. He'd read to her often, usually poems about the sea. *Sea Fever* and *Cargoes*, and *The Yarn of the Nancy Bell*, which always made us giggle, and Mick's favourite – *The Rime of the Ancient Mariner*. She'd sit back in her chair and read them to us, and every time her words would take us again down to the sea. Fifty years or more later I still love all of them, and *The Rime of the Ancient Mariner* is the one I love best. I know it by heart, start to finish. Every time I read it, and I read it often, I can hear her voice in my head. She wrote her own poems too she told us, but that she did in private, and however much we badgered her to read them to us, she never did. "My poems are like a diary," she said, "and for no one's eyes but mine."

Aunty Megs was an intensely private person. You always knew when you'd asked one question too many, like when Marty was looking at the photo on the mantelpiece of Mick in his sailor's uniform holding the hand of a little boy. When he asked her who he was, she didn't reply. When he asked once more, she said. "No one you know, and no one I know either." And the sudden coldness in her voice made it very clear she was going to say nothing more about it. We always thought it must have been her son of course, but we never dared to ask her ever again.

There really was so much that was wonderful at Aunty Megs', so much that changed my life. For a start we'd found a mother, and maybe as a result Marty and I became like real brothers there. We learned together how to build boats, only model ones maybe, but these model boats were the beginning of our lifetime love affair with the sea. We'd listen to Aunty Megs reading her sea poems, and talk long into the night about how we were both going to go to sea and be sailors like Mick had been. And I learned *The Ancient Mariner* by heart and recited it for Aunty Megs on her birthday. She listened with her eyes closed, and when they opened after I'd finished they were full of tears and full of love. Marty said it wasn't bad, but that I'd made a mistake and left out a verse. So I threw the cushion at him and he threw one at me. We both missed, and then all three of us were laughing. Henry came bustling in then to see what the noise was all about, took one look at us, decided we were mad, picked up the cushion, turned and walked right out again. I was happier in that moment than I'd ever been in all my life, happy as Larry.

Scrambled Eggs and Baked Beans

We'd been living at the Ark for about four or five years when Aunty Megs had her accident. Marty and I had been swimming in the river. We did that most days, when the weather was right, if there was enough water in the river. Swimming was something else Aunty Megs had taught us. "Almost as important as poetry," she'd say. "Best exercise there is. Could save your life one day too!"

We came wandering back up to the house, but when we

called for Aunty Megs she wasn't there. A quick look at the empty compound told us what she was doing and where she was. She'd gone off on one of her rides into the bush, hoping to release some of her little fellows, her family of animals. Normally she'd be gone for an hour or two, no more. But after several hours there was still no sign of her. We decided we shouldn't wait any longer, that we had to go out looking for her.

I was leading Big Black Jack out of the paddock when we saw her horse come galloping riderless down the track from the hills. We didn't waste any time then, but rode back up the way her horse had come, calling for Aunty Megs as we went. We knew roughly where it was she usually went to release her animals – the same area she'd found us all those years before. So that's where we headed now, both of us on Big Black Jack, Aunty Megs' horse following along behind. After a while we heard her singing, singing out loud – later she told us the singing helped to take her mind off her pain.

We found her out in the open beyond the trees, sitting with her back up against a rock, her family of animals scattered all around her. She was holding her arm tight to her chest, and had a nasty gash down one side of her face. There was so much blood all over her. Her shirt was soaked with it, both hands and her neck. She smiled up at us. "Am I glad to see you," she said. "Don't worry about the blood. Got plenty more where that came from. Just get me up and take me home, there's good boys."

She was already too weak to walk very far, so we knew that somehow we had to get her on to her horse. It wasn't at all easy. We had to find the right tree stump to use as a mounting block, then help her up into the saddle. I could see her shoulder was paining her dreadfully. I led the way on Big Black Jack while Marty rode up behind Aunty Megs, holding her steady in the saddle all the way home. Then I rode on into town for the doctor. It turned out she needed a dozen stitches in her face and that she'd broken her collar bone. He put a sling on her, and told her also that she'd lost a lot of blood and had to rest up for a while, a month at least, maybe more. She said, "Phooey."

The doctor stood there then, wagging his finger. "Don't you phooey me, Megs Molloy," he told her. "This is serious. You're to keep that sling on and stay still. These boys of yours'll look after you. You stay put, you hear me? Doctor's orders." And then he turned to us. "And if she tries to get up and go off looking for her little animals, you have my permission to lock her in." I think he was only partly joking.

Marty and I took him at his word. Now we were looking after Aunty Megs, which made a change. We made a deal with her. You tell us what to do and we'll do it, we said. But she had to stay put, stay still, rest as the doctor had told her. She agreed, reluctantly. So that's what happened. She only had to tell us what to do for a few days until we got into some kind of routine. After that we just got on with it. We took turns at everything we didn't much like doing – which was mostly the cooking and the washing up and the laundry.

Aunty Megs taught me from her sofa how to make scrambled egg on toast. She was very detailed and specific in her instructions. She allowed no deviation. Beat the eggs, bit of salt, bit of pepper, some milk. You had to spread the butter on the toast, keep it warm. Then you cooked the eggs, and the eggs had to be cooked just right, not for too long or they'd go all lumpy and tasteless. I did it better than Marty who always forgot the toast and burnt it. I still cook the meanest scrambled eggs in the world all these years later. It's still my favourite meal. During Aunty Megs' convalescence scrambled eggs alternated regularly with baked beans, or bubble and squeak, or corned beef hash. And we could fry bacon too. Poor Aunty Megs. Thinking back, it wasn't the best of diets for a patient, any patient. But she never grumbled. She laughed about it instead and told us in the nicest possible way that neither of us should ever take up a career in catering.

Outside though Marty and I really came into our own. We did everything that Aunty Megs had done. There was no time any more for swimming or fishing or climbing trees. Most mornings we'd go off, as she had done, up to the main road, searching for any surviving orphans. We fed those we had in the compound, and every so often we rode off into the bush, the animal cavalcade following behind, hoping one or two might stay up there. We milked the cows and the goats, fed the hens, took pot-shots with Aunty Megs' gun at any dingoes that came too close. We even learned to be brave with the geese, and to keep Henry out of the house – we were only partially successful in that. We learned to cope. And, to be honest, we liked it, every moment of it, even the laundry and the shopping.

We'd ride off once a week into town, one of us on Big Black Jack, the other on Aunty Megs' horse. We took it in turns to ride Big Black Jack because neither of us much liked Aunty Megs' horse. He was easily spooked, a bit nervous too, and not only by kangaroos either, but by just about everything. Whenever I rode him into town I felt the same as he did, always on edge, always twitchy. I could never forget that it was his fault Aunty Megs was lying there with a broken collar bone. He'd heard something rustling in the trees, she told us, and he'd reared up in sudden terror – that's how it had happened. I could never forget that, so I could never trust him.

Then there were the visitors who came to call, usually for tea. Aunty Megs didn't like these visits any more than we did. She swore she'd never fall off a horse again, nor ever get ill. It wasn't that she didn't like people. She did. But the trouble was they clearly liked her more than she liked them. Now she was incapacitated, they came visiting all too often and there was nothing much she could do about it.

When the vicar turned up, she didn't like it one bit, and didn't trouble to hide her feelings either. I was there when he came. She was pretty blunt with him. "I'm not at death's door yet," she told him. "Just broken a collar bone, that's all. No need for the last rites." He wasn't amused and went off quite quickly after that. And Marty and I didn't like the intrusion of these visitors much either. We felt that some of them were checking up on us to see if we were looking after her properly. They'd bring baskets of food, and all of them, without exception, would ask if there was anything they could do to help. We loved it when Aunty Megs told them that her boys were looking after her wonderfully, that everything was just fine.

It was about this time though that I first began to notice a change in Marty. He'd grown up a lot recently. He'd always been a lot taller than me, but now he seemed much older too. Until now I'd hardly noticed the four-year difference between us. But I did now. He was becoming the man of the house. Marty would sit with Aunty Megs for hours on end, listening to the stories of how her family and Mick's had come over to Australia from Ireland a century before, driven out by the potato famine, she said. They had found this valley and settled here. Marty loved looking through Aunty Megs' photograph albums with her too. He wanted to hear about Mick in particular, and she loved to talk about him too.

I remember sitting there watching them, and feeling a little jealous of Marty for the first time. Marty seemed to be able to talk to her in a way I couldn't. He wasn't just one of her "boys", he was becoming more of a friend. And she still treated me more like a boy, like a child. Up to now that had been fine, but suddenly it wasn't. Sometimes I couldn't bear to sit there and watch them, and I'd go off to bed early. It made me feel very alone again. I'd sulk about it from time to time, but with Marty I could never sulk for long. He wouldn't let you. One way or another he'd talk me round, get me smiling again.

Once we were alone in our room at night he would be the same old Marty again. We'd share our deepest secrets in the dark. We'd talk into the early morning sometimes. It was during one of those long nights that Marty told me his worst fear, which then became my worst fear too.

"D'you know what I think, Arthur?" he said. "Sometimes I think this is our real home, that we really are her children, that we'll be able to stay here for ever. Then I think: but we're not her children, are we? We're like her family of animals out there, her little fellows, her orphans. We're orphans too, aren't we? She hasn't said anything, but sometimes I think she wants us to go, just like she wants them to go. That boy in the photo with Mick. He's her real son. She won't say anything about him. But he must have gone, and when he went he didn't come back, did he? But I don't want to go, not ever. I feel like I'm a part of her proper family, that you're my brother, that Mick's my real father too. I'm going to be just like him one day. I am."

Then he added, "You've still got that lucky key of yours?" I had, though I didn't wear it any more – maybe because I thought I didn't need to. For some time I'd been keeping it in the drawer in my bedside table. I'd look at it from time to time, but it no longer seemed quite so important to me as it had been at Cooper's Station. I must have thought that I couldn't get any luckier anyway, so I just didn't need it any more. As for the cross Piggy Bacon had made us wear, I must have lost it. But I can't remember how or where. Marty chucked his in the river one day and I wondered then if he was throwing away his luck, our luck.

From that night on I couldn't get out of my head what Marty had said about Aunty Megs wanting us to leave one day. When we were alone, the two of us talked about nothing else. We decided to wait until Aunty Megs was up and about again, and then we'd ask her. But even after her shoulder was better and things were back to normal again, and she was doing the cooking and we were eating something else besides scrambled eggs and baked beans, we still kept putting it off. In the end we put it off for good. The truth is, I think, that neither of us really wanted to know the answer because we feared too much what it might be. It was to be another couple of years before we found out, and then we didn't have to ask her. Aunty Megs wasn't one to beat about the bush. When she told us, she told us straight.

"You're my Boys,
Aren't You?"

Aunty Megs had been quiet for a few days. She was like that. There'd be times when she seemed very preoccupied. She wouldn't sing. She'd sit alone on the verandah and read her poetry. She'd go for long rides. Marty said it was because she was missing Mick. And it was true that when his birthday came round or the anniversary of his death, that's when she went most noticeably quiet. But this time there was a difference. There was a nervousness about her we'd never seen before. It was almost as if she was avoiding us.

In retrospect, of course, we should have guessed what was coming, but we didn't. I put it down to Henry. Henry had gone missing a couple of days before. We weren't that worried, because Henry was always going off on walkabout into the bush, sometimes for a few hours, sometimes for a few days. He always came back. I'd just been outside to see if he was down his hole. I came in for supper and was washing my hands in the sink. "He's not back, Aunty," I said.

"Well, maybe he's gone for good this time," Aunty Megs was serving up as she talked. "Maybe Henry's finally decided it's the right time for him to go. 'Bout time too, I'd say." She took a deep breath before she spoke again. "Well, I reckon this is as good a time as any to tell you boys."

"Tell us what?" I asked, sitting down at the table. My plate was piled high in front of me with tatty pie – Aunty Megs' meat and potato pie with crusty pastry. I was longing to get at it, but we always had to wait till everyone was served. Aunty Megs was very strict about such things. "I've been writing letters," she went on, "to a friend of mine in Sydney – an old friend of Mick's from the navy, Freddie

Dodds. It's taken a while, but now it's all set up." Up until now she hadn't been looking at us, but now she was. "I decided to wait till you were both old enough, till you were both ready, and now I reckon you are. Freddie says you can start work in a couple of weeks' time."

My appetite for tatty pie had suddenly gone. Now we knew. Our worst fears were about to be realised.

"Freddie Dodds runs a boatyard, makes boats just like we do in the shed, only bigger of course, the real thing. He wants to take you on as apprentices. It's all fixed up. A proper paid job in the yard and a place for you to live."

While she was talking Henry nudged the door open, and came wandering in. None of us paid him any attention. "I'm not going to ask you what you think," Aunty Megs said. "But I am going to tell you why I'm doing this. If I've learned anything in this life, I've learned that you can't cling on. After Mick died, after I did my crying, I had to let him go. With all those animals out there in the compound, I mustn't hang on to them. They're not mine. They have a life to live out there. And you're not mine either. I have to let you go. You have a life to live."

Marty was on his feet, upset like I'd never seen him before. "But we're not dead. And we're not a couple of bloody joeys either. This place, it's our home. I don't want to go to Sydney. I don't want to go at all."

Aunty Megs went to him then, and put her arms round him and held him. "Do you think I want you to go?" she said. "Do you think I want to be here on my own? You're my boys, aren't you? The Ark is your home, always will be. It'll be here for you whenever you want to come back, and I'll be here too. I'm your mother, aren't I?" She turned to me then. "Don't just sit there, come and give your old mother a hug too." The hugging helped stem the tears after a while, but then the numbing reality set in. We were going. In a couple of weeks we'd be leaving home, leaving Aunty Megs.

We lived out those weeks as if every day was our last. They passed in a blur of riding and fishing and swimming. We groomed Big Black Jack every day till his coat glistened as never before. Henry was fed his bottle several times a day, spoiled rotten even more than usual. And all the while Aunty Megs was growing quieter and quieter. We so hoped she would weaken and let us stay, but she remained resolute. Every night she was darning or mending something. She couldn't have her boys going to Sydney looking like a couple of raggedy scarecrows, she said. And, while she was doing it, and because we knew she loved us to do it, we recited poems for her. Marty did *The Yarn of the Nancy Bell,* always his favourite because it had a rollicking rhythm and a gruesome twist to it at the end which we all loved. And I'd do my party piece, *The Ancient Mariner*.

The last time I did it, she looked up at me and said: "Thank you, Arthur dear, I shan't forget it." I haven't forgotten it either. She came into our room on the last evening, and put a book in each of our suitcases – mine was *The Rime of the Ancient Mariner*, Marty's, *The Yarn of the Nancy Bell*. I have them by me now, as I am writing this. They are still my most treasured books.

Out of a leather shoelace I made a new tie for my lucky key that night, and hung it around my neck. I wasn't at all sure I really believed in that kind of thing any more. At fifteen it seemed to me it might be a bit of a childish superstition, but I wasn't sure enough of myself to abandon it. Besides, the key was my last link to my sister, to the Kitty I remembered, or imagined. Memory or imagination? Already I couldn't be at all sure that Kitty had ever existed. Only the key told me she had. And the key had been lucky for us. Hadn't it brought us to Aunty Megs all those years before? So I kept my key. And I'm glad I did, very glad indeed.

The last I saw of Aunty Megs she was holding her straw hat on her head and standing there, disappearing into the cloud of dust left behind by the bus. For Marty and me this was the first time we'd been on a bus since the day we first arrived in Australia ten years before. Then we were leaving Sydney. Now we were going back. As I remember Marty said just about the same thing to me that he'd said then. "We'll be all right."

We sat silent the whole way, neither of us believing this was happening. Both of us knew we were leaving our childhood behind us for ever. It felt just like we were heading off into the bush again, into the unknown.

Together we might have been, but each of us felt very alone on that journey. When I felt the tears welling inside me, I tried to cheer myself up by thinking of Henry's horrible hat hole, or trying to get an *ee-aw* out of Barnaby. But sooner or later I'd think of Aunty Megs, and the moment that happened I'd be overwhelmed by a sadness I'd never felt before, a sadness so painful it gnawed at my stomach. I've only got to think about her even now, and I can feel the same pang, faint perhaps now like a distant echo, but still there. That's how much I loved her, loved our glowing time with her.

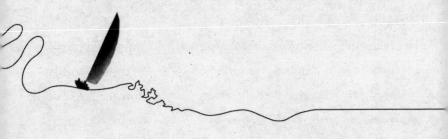

Freddie Dodds

Memory is a great and powerful magician. It plays tricks on you that you simply can't understand, no matter how hard you try to work them out. In my case it obliterated my early beginnings almost entirely, the lucky key around my neck being the only clue that I'd even had a beginning at all. And of my sister Kitty, the memory magician left me nothing but a shadowy phantom, which became more shadowy with every passing year. Yet I can remember the nightmare years of Cooper's Station and Piggy Bacon as if they all happened yesterday. But fortunately for my sanity, those healing, life-affirming years with Aunty Megs and Marty at the Ark are even more vivid to me than the nightmare time that preceded them.

I'm guessing now of course, but for me I think maybe it's partly at least a question of intensity. During those periods of my early life, maybe before I built up my protective wall around me as most of us do as we get older, I felt everything so strongly, so deeply. Good, bad or ugly, it stays with me. But that still doesn't explain why so much that has happened since those early years has been lost in a haze, that I seem to have forgotten as much as I've remembered. It's as if time itself had taken its time during my childhood, but once I got off that bus in Sydney it picked up speed, and from then on it was a roller coaster of a ride, and a bumpy one too, that brought me from then to now, leaving me with only fleeting moments of clarity, the highs and the lows, with so much in between, but lost to me for ever.

Freddie Dodds was there to meet us off the bus in Sydney. He drove us to the boatyard down at Newcastle. Mr Dodds – I never heard anyone call him Freddie except Aunty Megs – was the most silent person I ever knew. He wasn't unfriendly. On the contrary, he smiled a great deal, and he wasn't ever off-hand or cold. He just didn't say much, not to us, not to anyone. But he was a kind man through and through, and he ran his boatyard like a kindly ship's captain. He was the sort of captain that led by example, not by shouting at people. Everyone knew what they had to do and how to do it, and that included Marty and me.

We started out as general dogsbodies, sweeping up, fetching and carrying, making tea – we made an awful lot of tea. And we were nightwatchmen too. That was mostly because of where we lived. It paid our rent.

Marty and I lived on a boat just down the creek from the boatyard, a stone's throw, no more. It wasn't much of a place, a bit of an old wreck really, a forty-five foot yacht built in the 1940s that had seen better days, and was falling apart and beyond repair. But we didn't mind. It was home. We had a place of our own and we loved it.

No Worries she was called, and the name was perfect for her. And she was perfect for us too. We'd sit up there on deck in the evenings, the two of us, a cooling breeze coming in off the water, and up above us a sky full of stars. I've loved stars ever since. Down below we were as snug as a couple of bugs in a rug. Seventh heaven. What's more we were earning money. Not much, but it made us feel good, made us feel suddenly grown up. But however grown up we may have felt, we both missed Aunty Megs and the Ark, and Barnaby and Big Black Jack and Poogly and Henry. How we laughed about Henry.

The other blokes in the yard didn't treat us like that of course. To them we were just a couple of kids, particularly me, because I still looked like a kid. One or two of them would try to give me a hard time to begin with, but Marty was a good six feet tall now and big with it. He kept an eye out for me, they could see that. So they'd rib me a little from time to time, but that's all it ever was. We soon settled in and became part of the place. I became a bit of a mascot, I think.

We'd hardly ever see Mr Dodds. He'd be up in his office designing the boats. The place was full of his model boats, mostly yachts, and we'd only ever go up there to collect our money at the end of the week, or to pick up a letter from Aunty Megs perhaps. She didn't write often, but when she did her letters were full of news about Henry and Barnaby. It seemed now like news from another world.

It was while we were up there one day that he saw us

looking at the models of the yachts he'd made. "Megs tells me you can make models too," he said. And he showed us a design he was working on. "Do you think you can make this up for me?"

"Course," said Marty at once. I thought he was mad. We hadn't got a clue how to work from a design. We'd always had Aunty Megs alongside us in the shed back home. Now we were on our own. I didn't think we could do it. But we did. We learned fast because we had to. After work we'd sit down together at the map table in *No Worries*, and make the model of Mr Dodds' latest design. Eighth heaven now!

One way or another I've lived on boats more or less ever since, with a few prolonged and mostly unpleasant interruptions. I don't know what it is, why I love living on boats so much. Perhaps I just feel safe, like I am a part of the boat and she's a part of me. And I love the sound of the sea, the lapping of water above me, the movement below me, the clapping of the mast in the wind, and the birds. I love the birds. Ever since *No Worries*, I've woken up to the sound of seabirds. I could do without gulls mind. Dirty beggars. They always chose to park themselves on *No Worries*. There were dozens of boats all around to choose from and they always chose ours. And they didn't just leave *little* messages. Oh no! Marty didn't like cleaning up after them, so I had to do it. I didn't much like Marty while I was doing that, and I've hated gulls ever since.

But if I think about it, and I often have, my love of the sea must go back to Aunty Megs, and to Mick, her husband. He'd been a sailor. He'd built model boats. Then she did it because he had. Then we did it because she did it. She taught us all that poetry of the sea too, gave us our books, *The Yarn of the Nancy Bell*, and *The Ancient Mariner*, which we both knew by heart. So it's hardly surprising, I suppose, that Marty and I took to the sea like ducks to water.

Luckily Mr Dodds liked that first model we made. So we did the next one for him after that, and very soon we found ourselves working alongside all the other blokes in the boat-building shed, not dogsbodies any more, but like them, boat-builders proper.

Each of Mr Dodds' boats was a real marvel to me. They were mostly yachts, thirty-to-forty footers. You'd see her first as a sketch on his desk, then developed on the drawing board. Marty and I would make the model, and the next thing you knew – it took months, but it never felt like it – the next thing you knew, there she was in the water. A miracle every time it happened, a man-made miracle, that's what it was. For me it was like giving birth – as close as I ever got anyway! And Marty and I, and all the blokes in the yard, we were all so proud of them, like they were our children.

But their real father was Mr Dodds of course. I learned more about boats from Mr Dodds than I ever did from anyone else in all my life. There was never anything flash or fancy about his boats. They weren't built for speed or looks. They were built to sail. And that's the other thing I learned from Freddie Dodds. He didn't just teach us how to build boats, he told us how to sail them too. And that was to change my life for ever, and Marty's too.

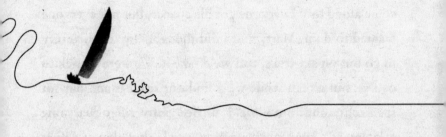

One January Night

I suppose there were about a dozen of us working in Mr Dodds' boatyard, including Marty and me, and by and large we were a pretty close-knit team. One or two came and went, but for the most part, people liked it and stayed. And that was largely because Mr Dodds treated everyone right. The money wasn't great – you could certainly earn more elsewhere in the fancier boatyards – but with Mr Dodds you got to build the whole boat, and best of all you got to sail it too. We had *job satisfaction* – that's what they call it these days.

Once a boat was finished, Mr Dodds would ask two or three of us to take her out on sea-trials. He would often come along too. Everyone got his chance, but not everyone wanted to do it. Marty and I did though. Any opportunity to go out on sea-trials, and we'd take it. We were seasick of course, but after a while we'd find our sea legs and our sea stomachs, and once we'd settled into it, it was raw excitement – hard work we discovered – but always a pure pleasure.

So, thanks to Mr Dodds, both of us got to know boats from the keel up, from the inside out. We built them and we sailed them too. And when we sailed we learned from Mr Dodds how to sail in harmony with the wind and the sea. He told us once that it was living at sea, surviving at sea, that taught him all he knew about boat-building. You have to understand the sea, he said, to listen to her, to look out for her moods, to get to know her and respect her and love her. Only then can you build boats that feel at home on the sea.

Every time we went out on a new boat with Mr Dodds, I learned that each boat we built was different, had a personality of her own. Once she's in the water she becomes a living creature, a unique creature. You ride her like you ride a horse. You have to know all her little quirks and fancies and fears, how she likes to ride the waves, how she likes to dance with the sea. That's what sailing is, a dance, and your partner is the sea. And with the sea you never take liberties. You ask her, you don't tell her. You have to remember always that she's the leader, not you. You and your boat are dancing to her tune.

I'm not sure how much Mr Dodds ever actually told us of all this. He was just about as monosyllabic out at sea as he was back in the boatyard. But one way or another we picked up his sailing philosophy and his boat-building philosophy, and it's stayed with me ever since. Everything I learned from him about the sea, about boats, has proved right. He was my sailing mentor, my tutor of the sea, a fine man and a fine seaman. The best.

He must have thought well of Marty and me too, because after about two or three years – Marty would have been about twenty-one by now, and I was seventeen – he called us up into his office and told us he thought we were ready to do one or two longer trips now, and on our own, just the two of us. We were young, he said, but he'd taught us well, he'd prepared us. A lot of the others didn't want to do the long trips – most of them had families to go home to. From now on he didn't just want us to trial his boats, he wanted us to deliver his boats to their new owners. As a result, Marty and I went all over – across to Hobart, up to the Whit Sunday Islands, and three times over to New Zealand.

It was on one of those New Zealand trips, to Auckland, that Marty first put an idea into my head, an idea that's been there ever since. We were sailing just off Dunedin. "You know what?" he said. "If we wanted we could keep going all the way to England. We could go and find your sister. You could find Kitty."

We never did, of course. But the idea stayed with me. Meanwhile, I was being paid for what I loved doing best, and I was doing it with my best friend on earth. Ninth heaven now. The two of us were becoming sailors through and through. And about that time, and partly because of the sailing I think, I stopped thinking of Marty as my elder brother, my bigger brother. The age difference between us that had meant so much at one time, and even set us apart a little for a while when we were younger, all but disappeared. On board the boats there was no skipper. We worked alongside each other, with each other, not younger and older brothers any more, but more like twins. We seemed to know instinctively what the other was thinking, what he was about to do. Our world had been the sea world for so long now. We'd shared so much. We'd been shaped by the same teacher.

Once a year for a couple of weeks' holiday we'd go back home to Aunty Megs, usually at Christmas. Sadly Henry wasn't around any more, but Barnaby was. Donkeys live longer than wombats. Barnaby still wouldn't *ee-aw* however much we tried to make him. We'd sit on the verandah the three of us together, and watch the sun go down, and we'd tell her all about the places we'd been and the boats we'd sailed. And on our last night we would all three of us recite *The Ancient Mariner*, for a few verses each until we finished it. When we had to leave at the end of the holidays, we never wanted it to end. We never wanted to come away.

Then one January night just after we'd come back from staying with Aunty Megs, our world turned upside down. We'd have both been in our early twenties by then. One way or another, it's been upside down most of my life ever since.

Thinking back, we should have read the signs. Just before

Christmas, Mr Dodds had laid off a couple of the blokes, and he hadn't been himself for some time. He'd been hiding away in his office, hardly showing himself. I thought he was probably just preoccupied with some new design – we all did. But there was no Christmas bonus that year, and no Christmas party in the boatshed either. We knew the boat business everywhere was going through a hard time, but we didn't realise just how hard until that January night.

I was asleep on *No Worries* when it happened. Marty had gone out for his last nightwatchman's check around the boatyard. It must have been about midnight, I guess. The two of us always took it in turns, and Marty was on duty that night. All you did was walk around the yard with a torch for half an hour. It was a routine neither of us liked much, but for doing it we were living on *No Worries* almost rent free, so we couldn't complain.

The first I knew of it, Marty was shaking me awake. I could see the flames straightaway through the skylight. I thought at first it was the boat that was on fire. When we got up on deck of *No Worries* you could see the whole boatyard was on fire from end to end. By the time we got down there, the fire fighters were already there. There was nothing they could do, nothing anyone could do. Luckily there were no boats inside. They were all out on the apron or in the water. Marty kept saying over and over that he'd only been down there an hour before and checked the place. He couldn't understand it. I saw Mr Dodds standing there still in his pyjama tops watching his whole world going up in flames before his eyes.

The police took Marty and me in and questioned us separately. I told them what I knew, which was nothing of course, except that each of us would go out last thing on alternate nights to check the boatyard, that we'd shared the nightwatchman duties for years and years. When they asked me whose turn it had been that night I told them that it had been Marty's. It was only after I'd said it that I realised what they might be thinking. I regretted it at once. But it was too late.

They arrested Marty that night on suspicion of arson. They wouldn't let me see him either. When I told Mr Dodds what the police had done, he just looked at me, then turned away without saying a word. It wasn't at all the reaction I had been expecting. I'd never known him to be heartless before. I couldn't understand it.

It turned out they were dead right about the arson, just wrong about Marty. I was wrong about Mr Dodds too, couldn't have been more wrong. He walked into the police station the next morning, and confessed to it all. Brilliant designer and boat builder that he was, good and kind man that he was too, it seemed he had got himself into a serious financial mess. It was an insurance scam. The poor man was trying to save his shirt. But once he'd heard they'd arrested Marty, he couldn't go through with it. Like I said, he was a good man. But they sent him to prison for seven years. Marty and I went to visit him, but they told us he didn't want to see anyone. We never saw him again. We tried again and again but he refused to see us every time.

So that was the end of the boatyard, the end of the good times, the happy times. One night was all it took for our whole world to fall apart. That one night in a prison cell for Marty was a night he never got over. I never got over it either. I felt I had betrayed Marty, that I'd locked him in that police cell as sure as if I'd turned the key myself. I told him how bad I felt but he never blamed me. "Forget it," he said. I couldn't. Marty was never quite the same after that night. Nothing was.

An Orphan Just the Same

They let Marty and me live on for a while on *No Worries*. By day we'd be out looking for work in other boatyards. But times were hard. There was just no work to be had in any of the boatyards in Newcastle or Sydney, nor anywhere else so far as we could discover, and boat-building was all we could do. Letters came from Aunty Megs saying we could always come home for a while if we wanted to, that there was always a place for us there, and plenty of work too. I can't believe how stupid we were not to have taken her up on her offer. I remember reading her letters over and over again, trying to decide whether to go. But for all sorts of reasons, Marty and I decided against it. He said, and at the time I thought he was right about it too, that you should never go back, that it'd be like giving up. And we both loved the sea, loved boats. We were determined to find work that kept us near the sea, or even on it preferably.

Those months we trudged the harbours and boatyards of Sydney looking for work took their toll on us both, but on Marty in particular. He was always the one who had kept me going through our most difficult times, ever since we were little. Now he just about gave up. I was the one who had to get him up in the morning when he wanted to just lie there. With every fruitless day, with every rejection, I watched him sinking deeper into the silence of despair. I tried to pull him out of it, to joke him out of it, tried to keep him positive. But it was no good.

Every night now he'd want to stay out drinking late. Time and again I had to drag him out of bars, and more than once he got into fights, usually over some girl. Drink did that to him. It didn't make him happy; it made him angry. Money, the little we had saved, was fast running out. Worse,

I could feel that the two of us were beginning to drift apart. Before we'd always done everything together. But now he'd go out in the evenings on his own. I could tell he didn't want me around. We never fell out, not as such. He was just going his own way and there was nothing I could do about it.

There was one morning when I couldn't get him out of bed no matter what I did. So I left him there and went off job hunting on my own. As usual I didn't find anything, but I was gone all day. When I came back home to *No Worries* in the evening, Marty had gone. I thought he'd gone out drinking, that he'd be back later. Even when a couple of policemen came the next morning, early, and woke me up, I wasn't that worried. I just thought he'd picked another fight and ended up in a police station for the night. I recognised one of the policemen – he'd interviewed me on the night of the fire.

I was half-asleep when they told me, so I didn't really understand, not at first. It was about Marty, they told me, and I had to come with them. I still couldn't understand. "We've got a witness who saw it happen," said the policeman I had met before, "someone who knew him. But all the same, we need you to come and take a look."

Then they told it to me straight. Marty had been drunk. He'd been doing the dinghy dance, leaping from boat to boat in the harbour, messing around. He'd fallen in, and just never came up again. They'd tried to find him, but it was dark. Then this morning a body had been found. I'm still trying to believe it happened. Even now, all these years later, the shock of it and the pain of it goes through me every time I think of it.

They took me to see him in the hospital. It wasn't Marty. It was just his body. I felt nothing then. I tried to feel something; I stayed there with him for hours. But you can't feel emptiness. They brought me back to *No Worries*, and I found Aunty Megs sitting on her suitcase waiting for me. It was the strangest thing. She'd woken up a couple of nights before and had known at once that we needed her. When I told her, all she said was, "I'm too late then."

There were just the two of us there for Marty's funeral. We buried his ashes up on the hill where the bushmen had left us that day, where Aunty Megs had first found us. I recited a few verses from *The Ancient Mariner*, ending with the line I knew he loved most of all: "Alone on a wide, wide sea". I'm glad I did that, because that poem is not just about a sea voyage, it's about the journey through life, and about the loneliness of that journey. It was the right thing to read.

Aunty Megs took me in again. She took care of me all she could. But now there were two spirits in that house with us, Mick and Marty. She had photos of them on the mantelpiece, side by side. But they were omnipresent, particularly, I remember, when we were sitting in silence together as we often did of an evening.

So much was the same. But so much wasn't. Henry's hole was still there under the verandah steps, still full of his beloved hats. Barnaby wandered the paddock shadowing Big Black Jack. The two had clearly become quite inseparable. But Aunty Megs' old horse had gone.

Aunty Megs and I still did everything the three of us had always done together. She didn't have the cows any more, just one nanny goat for her milk. But we still went up to the main road to rescue the orphan marsupials, her little fellows. We still kept them in the compound, and from time to time we'd make the long journey up to Marty's hill, as we called it now, to see if one or two of them would go back to the wild.

I had never been quite sure of Aunty Megs' age, but she must have been about seventy-five or eighty by now, and

I'd have been in my late twenties. As the years passed she stayed just as active in her mind, just as spirited. But as she said, her "poor old body doesn't work like it should". She didn't go out walking much these days. Her legs pained her. She never said anything much about it, but I could see it. She moved more slowly, more stiffly.

But she could ride all day though, and it wouldn't bother her a bit. On the contrary, she was happier up on a horse than anywhere else. She told me once that God had given her four legs to gallop with and a tail to whack the files with, that he'd just made a big mistake with the rest of the human race, that's all. And gallop she did too. Nothing she liked better. She said it made her feel alive. And I knew what she meant, because that's exactly how I'd felt out sailing with Marty on Mr Dodds' boats, with the wind in my face, and the sails straining above me and the salt spray on my lips. My longing for the sea never left me.

Aunty Megs had a good quick end, the best you can have, the doctor said when he came. She'd gone out with her torch to check her family of animals in the compound as she always did in the late evening. I was sitting, stargazing on the verandah when she came back. She sat down beside me, and said she thought she smelt rain in the air. Then she fell silent. I thought she'd gone to sleep – she'd often do that out on the verandah on warm evenings. And in fact that's just what she had done. She'd gone to sleep, but it was the long sleep, the final sleep.

The whole town came up to Marty's hill the day she was buried, and there were dozens of bushmen there too. I don't think I quite realised until then just how much she was loved. I put her ashes next to Marty's, a photo of Mick with them. When everyone left I stayed up there and recited the whole of *The Ancient Mariner* for them both. As I walked away I felt like an orphan all over again, a grown-up one maybe, but an orphan just the same.

Things Fall Apart

If there's one part of my life I'd like to forget entirely it was the next fifteen years or so. I suppose you could call them my years in the wilderness. I shan't enjoy writing about them, but I've got to do it. Like it or not, I can't just miss it out. Luckily for me, quite a lot of it is lost in a fog of forgetfulness. Perhaps that's what happens sometimes. Perhaps it's an automatic survival system that helps you muddle through. Maybe the memory just says: that's enough. I'm overloading with pain here and I can't cope, so I'm switching off. But it doesn't switch off entirely. So you remember, but thankfully only dimly, through the fog. Sometimes, though, the fog does clear, and you see the icebergs all around. You can hear them groaning and grinding and you just want to sail through the field of icebergs and out the other side, or you just long for the fog again. I'll tell you about the icebergs now. And like most icebergs are, they were unexpected and very unwelcome.

After Aunty Megs died I stayed on living at the Ark, doing what she'd done, living as we'd always lived. I didn't need much in the way of money. I had milk and eggs and vegetables. I lived a bit like a hermit. I rarely went into town and no one came to see me. I wasn't unhappy, not even lonely.

But then of course I wasn't alone. I had the animals, and like Dr Doolittle I talked to them. I think I talked to Big Black Jack more than I ever talked to anyone else all my life. He was probably over thirty years old by now, so I didn't ride him much any more. We'd go out for walks, the three of us – Barnaby, Big Black Jack and me. He'd walk beside me, his whiskery old face close to mine and we'd talk. Well, I'd talk. And I talked to the family of animals in the compound as well. Aunty Megs wouldn't have approved of it of course. You talk to them, you only gentle them she'd said. Gentle them and they won't survive in the wild. But they seemed to like me talking to them, and they went off when I released them just the same, and most of them didn't come back. So it was fine. Everything was fine, for a short while at least.

Then the strangest, saddest thing happened. I went out into Big Black Jack's paddock one summer morning, early, carrying a bucket of water to fill up their trough. I did it every morning, and usually Big Black Jack and Barnaby would come wandering over for a pat and a few words, and a drink of course. This particular morning they didn't come. So I went looking for them. I found Big Black Jack lying stretched out dead on the ground, with Barnaby standing over him, his head hanging. It took me all morning to bury Big Black Jack, Barnaby watching me all the time. He never drank a drop after that, never ate a thing, just stood by where I'd buried Big Black Jack and pined away. He was dead within a couple of weeks.

I was out there burying him in the paddock when I heard a car coming down the farm track. The man in the suit said he was a solicitor from Sydney. He was perfectly polite and proper. He simply told me that I'd have to move out. There wasn't any great hurry, he said. I could stay a couple more months. Then he told me something that shouldn't have surprised me, but it did nonetheless. Aunty Megs had had a son (the boy in the photo I'd seen all those years before, the boy she wouldn't ever talk about). There'd been a falling out years and years ago, the solicitor said, and they hadn't spoken since. Aunty Megs hadn't left a will, so everything she owned, the house and the farm and the furniture, it all went to her son. That was the law. The son it seemed wanted nothing to do with the property. He just wanted to sell it. Of course I could stay if I bought it. I told him I didn't have the money for that. Then I asked him what would happen about all the animals. He said they belonged to the son as well, everything did.

I didn't stay two months. I didn't stay two weeks. I stayed just a few days. That's all it took. I gave the nanny goat to the next-door farmer, and walked out into the bush every day with an ever-decreasing cavalcade of little animals following me. The last one to go was a joey. I've always wondered if I rushed him, whether he was quite ready. He was very small, but very independent minded. When he hopped off behind a bush, I turned and walked away quickly. I looked around once only, and he was gone. I hope he was all right.

I left the next morning, passed by the hill, Marty's hill, Aunty Megs' hill, to say my last goodbyes. I promised Marty I would go looking for Kitty one day, and I told Aunty Megs that all her family of animals were back in the wild now, where they belonged. Then I went on my way. I had a small suitcase, with a few clothes in it and one photo of us all together. And I had my lucky key round my neck. I did not look back.

I went to Sydney again because I had only one thought in my mind now: to go to sea. I got lucky – or so it seemed at the time anyway. I found a job straightaway on a fishing trawler. I didn't think twice. I just signed on. We'd be fishing the Southern Ocean, for tuna mostly. I didn't care what it was for. I was just so happy to be out there again, to feel the heaving seas about me, to watch the birds sailing the wind above me, to see the stars. You can see them better at sea than anywhere.

Then we began fishing. Most people have never seen a tuna that wasn't in a tin. I certainly hadn't, not before I went fishing for them. If they had, if they'd seen what I saw during the months and years that followed, they could never take the tin off the supermarket shelf, let alone eat the fish inside. A tuna is a beautiful shining creature, for me the most magnificent of all fish, and huge too. Day after day out on that trawler, I'd watch them lying there on the deck, suffocating to death, bleeding to death, thrashing about in their pain. And they weren't alone in their suffering: albatross, turtles, dolphins, sharks – they were all dragged up out of the ocean, and caught up in the slaughter.

No one seemed to mind what we were doing, just so long as we brought enough tuna back to port. And I didn't just stand by and watch. I was as guilty as everyone else. Massacre, murder, call it what you will, I was part of it. I played my part. But it paid well, and I was at sea where I wanted to be. I took the money. I stayed at sea. But I wasn't proud of myself, and the longer I stayed the more troubled I became by what I was doing. None of the others seemed bothered about it. On the contrary, the more we caught, the happier they were. They weren't bad blokes. They were just trying to earn a living like me.

We all got on well enough. When we weren't fishing or sleeping or eating, we were gambling. I liked gambling. I liked it a lot. I liked it too much. It made me feel like I was one of them. I was good at it too. And besides, it was totally absorbing. It took my mind off everything else. But each game was only a brief respite. Soon enough I was back up on that deck doing my killing.

I stuck it out as long as I could, but after a few years I'd had enough. Just the sight of another dying tuna made me feel physically sick. One night, on the way back to port, I was lying in my bunk unable to sleep. Every time I closed my eyes I could see a tuna thrashing about on the deck in its death agony. I knew I couldn't do another trip. I clutched my lucky key and swore to myself that as soon as I got back to Sydney, I'd do what I should have done years before, what I'd promised Marty I'd do. I'd go to England and look for my sister, Kitty. I had every intention of doing it too, but the others wanted a night out on the town, and I went along. By the time I left the casino in the early hours of the morning, every dollar I had earned was gone. There was no way I could pay the plane fare to England.

I find it difficult to explain to myself all these years later why I did what I did next. I think I must have had just three things on my mind – I needed money, and I still wanted more than anything to be at sea. And I didn't ever want to go fishing again. I remember walking down a street in Sydney, my suitcase in my hand. I happened to look up and saw a face smiling down at me from a poster. The man was in uniform, a naval uniform, and he looked just like Mick in that photo of him back at the Ark. He wore the same uniform too, the same peaked cap, the same Royal Australian Navy badge. The sailor inside the recruiting office – that's what it was – beckoned me in. It was as simple as that. And as usual, I thought my lucky key had done it again. I'd join the navy, I'd have regular money in my pocket, I'd be at sea. Perfect. I signed on the dotted line, and within a couple of months I was back on board ship, a very different kind of ship, a destroyer.

I never read newspapers much, hardly ever watched television either. I didn't pay much attention to the world outside, not in those days. If I had, maybe I would have seen it coming. A couple of years later and we were sailing off to war – the Vietnam war. Another kind of murder, but people this time, not fish.

The Centre Will Not Hold

Most of the world is now too young to remember the war in Vietnam. Wars become history all too soon and are forgotten all too soon as well, before the lessons can be learned. Which is why we have more wars, and always more wars. But they are not forgotten by those who fought in them. I don't forget the anger of our guns, the shudder that went through the ship when she was hit, the silence that followed and the cries of wounded men. They called it "friendly fire" afterwards. We were bombarded by our own side, an "unfortunate" mistake they told us. It felt a little more than unfortunate at the time. Good men died for nothing that day, and I was lucky not to be one of them.

These were times I do remember, only too well, but don't want to have to think about. I don't want to write about them either, but I can't pass by Vietnam as if it never happened, as if I'd never been there, been part of it. Not because I'm proud of it. On the contrary.

There were long months of boredom at sea, long nights sweating below deck. I can still remember how excitement turned to fear in my stomach when the guns first fired. I can still see Dickie Donnelly from Adelaide – we only just celebrated his eighteenth birthday – lying there on the deck, his eyes looking up at the sky above him and not seeing. There wasn't a mark on him. It must have been the blast that killed him. I was holding his hand when I felt the last breath of life go out of him.

But, apart from Dickie Donnelly, most of the dying in that war was done far away, on the shore. I discovered it's a whole lot easier to do your killing when you're miles away from your target. You're in your ship, way out at sea, and you just fire the guns. You don't see where the shells land.

So you don't think about it, because you don't have to, at least not to start with, not until you come face to face with it. After Dickie Donnelly, I couldn't put it out of my mind. This was what our shells were doing to the enemy, to the Vietcong, to the North Vietnamese. They'd be young lads, just like Dickie, with mothers and fathers, sisters and brothers, an enemy I'd never even seen. And I was firing the guns that did it. All I'd ever done while I'd been at sea, it seemed to me, was killing.

I couldn't wait for the war to end, to get out of the navy. Sickened and sad I turned my back on the sea, for ever I hoped. I had come to hate the sea, the place I'd always loved, where I'd always longed to be. For me the sea had become a place of blood.

I went inland after the navy, bummed my way around, picking up any work I could find. I went gold mining in Western Australia, worked on a cattle station in the Northern Territories, spent most of my time branding cattle. I did seasonal work picking grapes in vineyards outside Adelaide, in the Clare Valley it was. And after that, I was a jackaroo for a while on a sheep station near Armidale in New South Wales. After that I never wanted to look at another sheep in my life. Back-breaking work, smelly work. At times I felt like I was back on Cooper's Station.

I couldn't settle anywhere, not for long. I kept moving on, moving on. I wasn't leaving anywhere. I wasn't going anywhere. I was just drifting. I still wore Kitty's key around my neck, never took it off, not once. But I'd long since stopped believing it was lucky. I wore it, mostly out of habit, and maybe because I still thought that I might one day be able to go back to England and find Kitty, find out if she'd ever existed even, find out what the key was for.

But I never did it, and I know why. I was frightened, frightened of discovering the worst – that she never had existed, that I'd made her up so as not to feel entirely alone in this world. I still thought about the key, though, when I caught sight of it in the mirror as I was shaving. I thought about it every time I touched it. But any real hope I had harboured of actually ever doing anything about it was fast fading, along with my sanity. My centre would not hold.

I don't know why it happened when it did. None of it really makes much sense to me even now. If there was a physical cause that triggered my troubles – and when it comes to health, I don't think body and mind can be separated – then it might well have been lack of sleep. No matter how exhausted I was after a day's work, I couldn't get to sleep. I'd lie there, not tossing and turning, just thinking. And no matter how hard I tried, my mind kept coming back to it. It was always the killing. It was the shining tuna lying on the deck bleeding, fighting for life, Dickie Donnelly's last breath warm on my hand.

But there was another picture there that haunted me, that would not go away every time I closed my eyes. I'd seen it first as a black and white photo in a magazine, I think, then in a film on the television. It was an image of a young girl in Vietnam, running down the road away from her village. She had been burned by napalm bombing, dreadfully burned. She needed help. She was coming towards me. She was naked and she was crying. And she kept coming towards me, holding out her arms to me, and suddenly her face would be Kitty's face. I knew I'd been part of the war that had done that to her, to a girl just like Kitty and to thousands and thousands of others too. Every night she was there, and every night I couldn't sleep.

I'd be late for work in the morning, or I'd fall asleep on the job. I'd get the sack. Time and again I got the sack. Any money I did earn I'd gamble away the same day I got it. I'd hitch a ride anywhere and had no idea where I was when I arrived nor why I'd gone there. I felt myself slipping into a deep dark hole of despair. I couldn't find any way of stopping myself, and in the end I didn't even want to stop myself. It seemed a lot easier just to give up and let go. So I did.

I woke up in hospital. They told me I'd drunk a bottle of whisky, and taken a lot of pills. The doctor said I was lucky. Someone had found me in time. I didn't think I was lucky at all. He wanted to keep me in hospital, for my own safety, he told me. I'd had a breakdown, he said. It was an illness like any other, and I'd have to be hospitalised until the treatment was over. I gathered pretty soon that it was the kind of hospital you could leave only when the doctor said you could. I looked out of the hospital window and saw the sea. I asked where I was. "Hobart, Tasmania," he said. When he went out he locked the door behind him, just as Mr Piggy had at Cooper's Station. I was a prisoner again.

So there I was, over forty-five years old by now, rock bottom, suicidal and losing my mind in some hospital in Hobart, and I don't remember to this day even how I got to Hobart. But I still had Kitty's key around my neck. The doctor asked me a lot about my childhood. I showed him my key, and told him about Kitty too. He asked if I hadn't made Kitty up entirely. Hadn't I invented her because I so much wanted her to exist, wanted to have a family?

He was a strange man, my doctor. He never smiled, not once. But to be fair to him he didn't get angry either. And I gave him enough cause to get angry. Thinking back, I treated the poor man a bit like a punch bag. He didn't seem to mind, just let me rant on. Nothing rattled his professional calm. I had the strong impression he didn't believe a word I told him. And I don't think he cared much either. So after a while, I didn't tell him anything more. We'd sit there having long silences together, and I'd gaze out of the window at the sea and watch the boats.

It was during one of those silent sessions that I felt the stirrings of a new longing. I wanted to build boats again, and to sail them. I'd sit in my room and recite *The Ancient Mariner* aloud over and over again. It made me feel I was out there at sea, and it reminded me of Marty and Aunty Megs. And I remember too that I'd sing *London Bridge is Falling Down* very loudly in the shower. I loved my showers, and singing made them even better. I was sad and alone, very alone, grieving for everyone I had loved, everyone I had lost.

Then one morning there was this new nurse on the ward who smiled at me, not because she was trying to be kind but because she *was* kind. She treated me like a person not a patient. My whole world lit up every time I saw her. I was mesmerised, and not just by her gentle beauty and her shining black hair. It was the sound of her laughter, her sheer exuberance that lifted my spirits and made me feel lonely without her. When I told her about Kitty's key, about Cooper's Station and Marty, and Aunty Megs and Vietnam, she listened, and she wanted to know more. When I recited *The Ancient Mariner* to her, she listened. Bit by bit, every time I saw her, I felt myself coming together again. I made a model boat for her, a liner with three red funnels. I was beginning to see a way out of my darkness. And once I could see the light, then I knew I could climb up towards it.

So that's what I did, and when I walked out of that hospital a couple of months later, my nurse was waiting for me. Zita, she was called. And I knew as she drove me away that morning that she was all I'd been looking for all these years. I found more than happiness with Zita. I found myself again, then a home too, and an entire family. Best of all, I now had a reason for living.

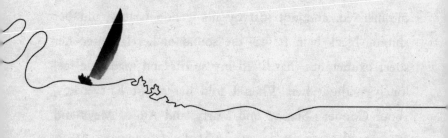

Oh Lucky Man!

What Zita had done was to restore my faith, and not just my faith in myself, but in the wider world around me too. When you're down and out you get to thinking only how bleak and brutal the world is. The more you believe it, the more you expect things to be like that, and the more they prove to be like that. It's a self-fulfilling prophecy. That's the spiral I was in. What Zita has shown me since the day I first met her is that the world is not like that, most people are not like that, I'm not like that. She didn't do it by telling me, by preaching to me, but just by being who she is. Genuinely good people are like that. The sun shines out of them. They warm you right through. Zita's like that. As the song goes – and songs do get it right sometimes – when she smiles, the whole world smiles too. She was half my age and she chose me to love. If she hadn't told me first, I'd never have dared to tell her back. Oh lucky man!

She came from a family of smiling people. That's where she took me the day we drove away from the hospital, to her family home down by the seashore in Hobart. There was a whole tribe of them, the most extended family I'd ever met, Greeks all of them, Cretans, dozens of them and loud with laughter – when they weren't crying that is. They are people of extremes, wonderful people. They welcomed me at once as one of their own, and that meant everything to me. I was Zita's man, so I was part of the family, no questions asked. They were all open-hearted and whole-hearted. The children climbed on my knees that first lunchtime. They tugged me by my fingers towards the sandpit or the swing or the beach. They'd found a new great big puppy to play with. I laughed with them in the sunshine, just as I'd laughed with Marty at the Ark all those years before.

From that day on I knew I had a proper home and a proper family of my own. And I danced, for the first time in my life I danced. Cretan dancing. Zita taught me, tutored me through the awkward stage where my feet simply refused to step to the music, told me to feel the music, to let the music do it. It worked. But I'll never dance like a Cretan, like Zita. You can see the music floating through her. She's a wonder to watch.

But there was more. Zita hadn't mentioned it before. Maybe she left her father to tell me himself. "Zita she say you likes boats, Arthur," the old man said after lunch as we walked together by the seashore. He had a truly wonderful white moustache which he stroked often, not out of affectation but rather out of affection, I think. There was a glint in his eye that demanded and expected an answer. You didn't have conversations with Zita's father. He talked, you listened.

"Me too," he went on. "I likes boats. I grow up with boats when I was little boy on Crete. Now I have my own boatyard. Stavros Boats. Now I build my own boats – big ones, little ones, fat ones, thin ones, anything that sell. And I build good boats too, the best boats. We all build boats, the whole family. You can help us, yes?" He didn't wait for a reply. "That's good, that's good." He stopped then and turned to me. "I want Zita to marry a good Cretan boy, young and strong. But she say she want to marry you. Zita, she like her mother – you don't argue with her. So you're not Cretan boy – that's not your fault. And you're not young – that not your fault either. She like you and you likes boats – that's good enough for me."

I was like the cat that got the cream and fell on his feet all at once and the same time. And it got better too. Within a month or two I was married to Zita, and I was designing all the old man's boats for him, and making models for the children too. We lived all together in the huge family home adjoining the boatyard, where everyone had their own chair on the verandah – even me, my wedding gift from Zita's father.

Then came the icing on the cake. I know you're not supposed to mix metaphors, that cats that get the cream and icing on the cake hardly seem compatible. But to describe this supreme moment of my life, I need all the metaphors I can lay my hands on – there's another one! Before I knew it, Zita and I had a little girl of our own, Allie – Alexis really, but I've never called her that. Everyone else does, but to me she was always Allie.

"She's got your nose," Zita told me. Luckily for me that's all she's got of me. The rest is perfect. I have to say that because it's Allie who's writing my story down at this moment, typing this all out for me on her word processor. But it happens to be true. She types as fast as I can speak, which is amazing. But then she's always been amazing to me, ever since she was born nearly eighteen years ago. It seems like yesterday.

Down in the old man's boatyard, I was adapting Mr Dodds' designs for ocean-going yachts, for dinghies, for motor boats too. For the first time now I had the opportunity to imagine a boat, to dream it up first in my head like a story, then sketch it and design it and build it. But all the while I kept Mr Dodds' principles in mind: that a boat should be built to dance with the sea, not just to go fast or look sleek. I had one or two arguments with my new father-in-law about this, but as soon as he found my designs were selling well, he was more than happy to let me do what I wanted.

One boat I conceived, designed *and* built all with my own hands. I never let anyone else go near it or even see it till I'd finished it, and then the first person to see it was Allie. I called her *Kitty*. It came into my head – it just seemed a good idea at the time. And Allie liked saying it over and over. So the name stuck. *Kitty* was bright yellow, and built to sail the roughest waves in Allie's bath, to survive close encounters with all her plastic ducks and loofahs. Based as usual on one of Mr Dodds' designs, *Kitty* was sturdy and sound, the most bath-worthy boat ever built. Allie couldn't turn that boat upside down even if she wanted to – and she tried often enough. Turn Kitty over and she'd just pop right back up again.

When she grew bigger, I built her a bigger boat, *Kitty Two*, I called this one, to sail on the pond, yellow again and fully rigged. Mr Dodds' designs, I discovered, worked every bit as well in the sea or the pond or the bath. And just as soon as she could walk, I made her first real sailing boat, a dinghy, *Kitty Three*. This one was big enough for the three of us to go sailing together in her. Once, on Christmas Day, Allie insisted on taking the tiller so I let her. As she took us out to sea that day, she began singing her favourite song *London Bridge is Falling Down*! Can't think who taught her that!

Allie was a natural sailor – it came I'm sure from starting so young. I hardly had to teach her at all. She took to it instinctively, and loved every minute of it. She won her first race when she was six. She just lived for her time on the water. Every day after school she'd be down at the boatyard, not only watching either, but building. For her, the boatyard was the next best thing to the sea, and she often had a canny way of making the one thing lead to another.

She learned boats the proper way, Mr Dodds' way, my way: from the keel up, from the inside out. And she learned the sea, because she was always out there. I'd go with her when I could of course, but if I couldn't then she'd pester someone else in the yard. She wasn't at all easy to say no to, not for me, not for anyone. Even the old man, her grandfather, who was no one's soft touch, was putty in her hands. Zita used to say Allie had us all round her little finger, and that was just about right. But she was clever with it too. She knew she had to put in the hours down at the boatyard. Whatever needed doing she'd do it. She was the same kind of dogsbody Marty and I had once been in Mr Dodds' yard. She was a hard worker, and the blokes saw that and liked it, which was why one way or another she'd usually manage to get one of them to take her out sailing.

It was seeing her so at one with her boat, so happy, that inspired me to take it up seriously again myself. Watching the joy on her face, the sheer exhilaration, was infectious. I discovered I didn't just enjoy sailing because she was with me, I began to love it again for itself, the way I had before. I was loving it because it made me feel alive again like nothing else. True, the sight of a passing fishing trawler, the unmistakeable lines of a warship on the horizon could still trouble me. But it was the heady, happy days with Marty I remembered most. And now I was out there again alone or with my own daughter. Zita came out with us only rarely on what she called picnic days, when the sea was listless, when there was so little wind the sails hung there limp above us. She liked it best like that, but Allie and I were bored out of our minds.

It was on one of those picnic days that it happened – Allie would have been about ten by then I think. The three of us were lazing there in the sun after lunch. I had my eyes closed when I felt Allie fiddling with my lucky key. She loved doing that. "Tell me about the key again, Dad," she said, "and your sister Kitty." I'd told her the story hundreds of times before, trying to make it a little bit more interesting each time, as you do. This time when I'd finished, she took it off me and put it round her neck. "You know what we should do when I'm a bit older, Dad? We should sail to

England and find her. Could we do that, Dad?"

That was exactly what Marty had said I should do all those years ago as we were sailing past Dunedin off New Zealand.

"Could we, Dad?" Allie asked again.

"It's a long old way to England," I told her. "Half way round the world. And what if we can't find Kitty when we get there? I've no idea at all where she'd be."

"We could find her," Allie said. "Course we can, and we'll find out what the key's for. I think it's a box. Got to be, hasn't it? S'only a little key. And we'll open it up. What's inside, d'you think?"

And then I said it. I said it quite deliberately. I'd thought about it, and I meant it. "I don't know what's inside," I replied. "But we're going to find out, Allie. I'll have to build a bigger boat of course, but I can and I will. We'll sail to England and we'll find Kitty. If she's there we'll find her. It's something I should've done a long time ago."

"Do you promise me, Dad?" she said, looking up at me wide-eyed with excitement.

"I promise you, Allie," I replied. And it was a promise I was determined to keep.

I looked across at Zita then, and she knew I meant it too.

I could see she was suddenly fearful. But I couldn't backtrack now. I'd promised. Everything had been decided in those few moments. When Allie was older, we'd do it. We'd sail to England together and find my sister, Kitty, and discover what my lucky key was really for. On the way back home that evening, I was already designing the boat in my head – *Kitty Four*, she'd be called.

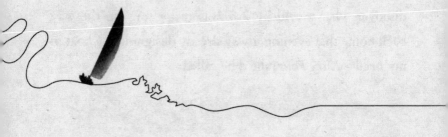

Kitty Four

It could have been just a pipedream. It would have been if Allie hadn't kept me up to the mark. She didn't pester me – not exactly. But she did prod me, and every prod was a reminder, and all the reminders served to crank me up, to get me going, make me feel guilty if ever I was thinking of back-sliding – she knew me too well, she still does. She knew the dream of the boat, the dream of her great ocean adventure, would never come to anything unless she made it happen, unless she made me do it. I had my own reasons for delaying the commitment, and they weren't just backslides. I had good sound reasons too.

Both she and I needed far more experience of ocean sailing before we could embark on such a voyage – Zita was adamant about that. There was no way she'd let us go, she said, unless she was quite sure we were both ready for it. The old man said the same.

"Yous not going till I say yous ready," he said. And he always meant what he said.

Zita also made it absolutely clear that Allie couldn't go until she was eighteen – and that was years ahead. But years have an uncanny knack of passing. The boat I was building in my head was a thirty-three footer – the ideal size for ocean sailing, Mr Dodds used to say, because it's compact. "Size," he once told me, "is not all it's cracked up to be. Look at what happened to the Titanic." And while I was busy dreaming up my compact thirty-three footer, I was out there practising hard – encouraged by Allie, who was herself entering and winning every race she could.

I knew what she was about. With every new silver cup on the mantelpiece she was proving to us all just how good a sailor she was. Zita was proud of her and her grandfather was too, too proud I sometimes felt, but then grandfathers are entitled. But neither was happy about the prospect of the two of us going off around the world. They made that very clear. And already Allie was talking of not just going to England and stopping off there to find Kitty, but of doing the whole thing, the entire circumnavigation.

As for me, I won no silverware, but I was in training. Four times I went crewing on the Sydney–Hobart race, and of course, everyone at home was there to see me off, follow my progress on the television, and was there to welcome me when I came home. I had some hairy moments – the Sydney–Hobart race specialises in providing those. No boat I sailed in ever won. But for me that wasn't the point. I was learning again everything I'd learned with Mr Dodds and Marty, and more besides. I could feel my confidence and strength growing with every race. Best of all though, and thanks to Allie's persistence and dogged determination, the old man himself was coming round. He was still cautious, but he was beginning to encourage us now in our great endeavour. Allie had it in her blood, he said. Cretans were the greatest and bravest sailors in the world.

When I told him I needed some time off work to do

some longer sails on my own he arranged, just as Mr Dodds had done before, for me to deliver Stavros boats far and wide. I sailed again to New Zealand, solo this time. I took a boat to Bali once, with Allie, and another to Hong Kong, solo again this time. On each trip I was testing my endurance, learning how to deal with minor and major catastrophes alike, and all the time I was learning the sea again, learning the winds and the tides. I was ready. I was as ready as I was ever going to be.

By now Allie was sixteen. The two of us had done lots of sailing together, ocean-going, long trips. I knew how good a sailor she was – far better than me already, that's for sure. She only had to feel the wind and to look at the waves to understand what dance they wanted to do, what sails were right; she had already mastered all the new gizmos of modern sailing. That side of it seemed to come as naturally to her as the sailing itself. When she was on board I spent most of my time cooking or watching albatross or dolphins, or stargazing. I just wasn't needed. But she was still only sixteen. Still Zita wasn't at all happy about it. And still we didn't have a boat.

We had a design though by now, and just as importantly, we had the means to build it. The old man had done a deal with me. He'd sponsor the whole thing, he said, pay for everything down to the last can of baked beans. But he wanted the Stavros Boats' name and the logo up there on the sails, and along the sides. And he insisted we had to get as much publicity as possible.

"We can sell many many boats on the backs of this," he said.

"Just so long as we can call the boat *Kitty Four*," I told him.

"You calls it what you like," he said. "Just make it the safest boat you ever built in your life. And you brings my little Allie back to me safe and sound, you hear me?"

By now of course everyone down at the boatyard was part of the great project. We all built the keel together. Everyone rallied around and helped, all of us fired by Allie's energy and enthusiasm. They all knew her well – after all she'd been hanging around the boatyard ever since she was knee-high. They'd watched her grow up and now they wanted to be part of her dream, wanted to help make it come true. They all knew the story about the key I wore around my neck, and about my sister, Kitty. Everyone in the boatyard felt they were part of the same story. Better than that, they were making it happen. Never was a boat built with so much care and affection as *Kitty Four*. We all wanted to build the safest boat that ever sailed the ocean. Knock her down and she'd come back up. Turn her over and she'd right herself again. She had to be unsinkable; we'd make her unsinkable.

Allie worked alongside the rest of us in the shed, late into the night for months on end. Zita allowed her do it only if she kept up with her school work. She was very strict about it. So Allie did both. Keeping Zita on side was the most difficult part of the whole thing. As the skeleton of the keel began to look like the beginnings of a real boat, as Allie's eighteenth birthday came ever closer, as plans for the trip began to crystallise, she worried more and more. Both Allie and I did all we could to allay her fears, to convince her that we'd be fine. But night after night, she'd lie awake beside me. I tried to reassure her about how safe the boat would be, how we'd make sure everything was just as it should be, about how good at sea Allie and I were together. We'd been in big seas, we'd managed, we'd coped, we'd be fine. Telling her though wasn't enough.

It was Allie who came up with the idea that at last enabled Zita to feel a little happier about it. She gave her a part in it all, a vital part. She told her we were going to need someone to run the whole communications side for us back home, all the emails, Satphone, the website. Allie said she would teach her everything she needed to know. That seemed to make all the difference. As we finished the keel down in the boatyard, Allie and her mother worked together at home. They converted the box-room to a communications room, fitted it all out, bought all the computers and gizmos they needed.

We were all there together to see *Kitty Four* go into the water for the first time. Zita launched it for us. "I name this boat *Kitty Four*. May she take you both to England. May you find Kitty, Arthur, and all you're looking for. And most of all, may she bring you back home safely." I saw a lot of grown men cry that morning, and I was one of them. So was the old man. Allie held my hand tight as we watched.

"Thank you, Dad," she whispered. "She's going to be the best boat, the best boat in the world. I know she is."

That evening as we celebrated I knew something wasn't quite right. I felt dizzy first, then there was a pain in my head that wouldn't go away. I'd always felt fit as a fiddle before, so when I fainted the next morning, Zita called the doctor. So the saga began – the tests, the waiting, more tests, more waiting, then the results, the verdict. The doctor gave it to me straight, because I asked him to. I had a brain tumour – malignant, advanced, aggressive. There was nothing they could do. Surgery wouldn't help.

Radiotherapy wouldn't help. Chemotherapy wouldn't help. Nothing would help. When I asked how long I'd got, he said, "Months."

"How many?"

"Five or six, difficult to be precise about it. I'm sorry."

"So am I," I said.

Since that day I've had so much to think about, so much to get sorted. I told Zita that I didn't want to talk about it, didn't want anyone to know outside the family, that I just wanted everything to go on as normal as possible, for as long as possible. Without Zita, without Allie, and without *Kitty Four* I would have fallen apart. I know that.

We finished her together, fitted her out just as Allie wanted her. I wanted to see her in all her yellow glory – yellow she had to be, Allie said, because all the other *Kitty*s had been yellow, and they'd been yellow because all the foods she most loved as a little girl were yellow – custard and butter and bananas. I was there on the quayside to see Allie take her out for the first time, saw her dancing through the waves, and I knew I'd never built a finer boat.

There was something else I had to do as well before I went. I had to talk it all out, write it all down, everything I could remember right up until now. To start with I could manage to write well enough on my own, but as things got worse, as my sight gave up on me, I've had to dictate it. I prefer it that way anyway. Telling a story is so much easier for me than writing it. Some of it I've dictated to Zita, but sometimes I can tell she finds it hard to endure. That's why Allie and I are finishing it together.

So in the end we didn't sail around the world together, but we have sailed around my life together. Allie told me yesterday that she's talked it over with her mother and the old man and they've given their permission. She says she's going to sail to England on *Kitty Four* on her own now, that when she gets there she's going to do all she can to find my sister Kitty and tell her all about me and find out about my key, Kitty's key. And then she's going to sail back all the way home again. Zita and her grandfather are still a bit sticky about it, she says, but they'll come round. They will too. She's quite a girl, my Allie, quite a girl.

There's times I think she only told me that to make me happy. But when Allie says something she always means it – she's very like her mother that way, very like the old man. So I think maybe she really will do it. The thought that Kitty and Allie might one day meet up makes me very happy – my real world meeting my dream world. It's just a pity I won't be there to see it, that's all. Or maybe I will be. Who knows.

As I said at the beginning, I knew the ending of my story before I began telling it. But maybe it isn't quite the ending, not yet. I'll live on for a while in Zita's memory and in Allie's memory. I'll be part of their lives for as long as they live, just as Marty and Aunty Megs have always been part of mine. This story of mine will help me live on a little longer. And I want that. I want that very badly. Living a little longer is suddenly the most important thing in the world for me.

But this is the end of the story, the story of me. What will happen to me soon is the end of everyone's story. Not a happy ending, not a sad ending. Just an ending. Time to say goodbye.

By Arthur Hobhouse,
(brother of Kitty, and Marty, son of Aunty Megs, husband of Zita, father of Allie.)

PS This story is dedicated to Zita. Kitty's key and my copy of The Ancient Mariner are for Allie to keep.

Part Two

The Voyage of
the *Kitty Four*

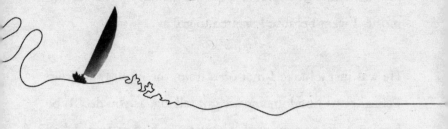

What Goes Around, Comes Around

I always liked messing about with boats, and *in* boats too. As Dad said, I'd been doing that just about all my life, from the bath to the Southern Ocean. I think I was born to sail, and I mean that. So when I set out on my great sailing adventure, it was because I wanted to do it. I'd been dreaming of doing it for almost as long as I could remember. I didn't do it just because I promised Dad I would. That was only part of it. Yes, Dad had built the boat for us to sail to England together, to find Kitty together. And yes, it's true that I try very hard to do what I say I'm going to do, to keep my promises. So of course I went in memory of Dad, but mostly I went because I wanted to go.

He was just a bloke I met on a train, the night train from Penzance to London, and we got talking, as you do. To be honest, I didn't pay much attention to him at first. I had my laptop out, and I was busy writing emails to Mum and Grandpa. Besides, I didn't want to talk. I was tired. I wanted to get my emails done and then have a good night's sleep. But we just got chatting. No, that's not quite true. He started chatting, and I listened. I think I listened because he was funny, and because he was Australian, the first Australian boy I'd talked to face-to-face in months. He rattled off his entire life history in about a minute, before the train even left the station.

He was called Michael McLuskie. Born in Sydney, went to school in Parramatta. Hated it. Spent all the time he could on the beach, surfing. Left school. Decided he'd go round the world searching out all the best surfing beaches he could find. Came to England, to Cornwall, to Newquay and St Ives. Big mistake. No one told him they didn't do proper waves in England. You could find bigger waves in a teacup, he said. He'd spent the last couple of months sitting on drizzly grey beaches waiting for waves, and now he'd run out of money. He was going home, to sunshine, to Australian surf, the real kind, the rolling kind, the thundering curling kind, the riding kind.

"You surf?" he asks me.

"No," I tell him. "I sail."

"Same thing."

"No, it's not."

"Have a Mars bar," he says.

And that's how it all began, with an argument and a Mars bar. Six years on and we still argue from time to time, not that often. But when we do, we often patch it up by sharing a Mars bar. It helps us remember that train journey, the time we first met. It makes us smile, and it's really hard to argue if you're smiling. I know because I've tried.

"So what about you?" Michael says.

"What about me?"

"Well, I've told you the story of my life, so now you've got to tell me yours."

"You're just chatting me up," I tell him.

"Yes, I am," he replies, "but tell me all the same. It's a long journey."

He was right about that. It was going to be about eight hours through the night, and the seats were uncomfortable, so sleeping wouldn't be easy. And besides, he was very persuasive.

"What happened to your arm?" he says.

I'd almost forgotten I had my arm in a sling. I'd already got used to it like that. "It's a long story," I tell him.

"I'm listening," he replies, flashing me his wide white surfer's smile. "And you can tell me your name too if you like."

I told Michael my story (and my name) that night because I liked him. There, I've said it, and that's the honest truth of it. To begin with I thought, *I'll do what he did, just rattle through my whole life history, get it all over with as quickly as possible.* But once I'd started it didn't work out like that, and that was because he kept trying to draw more out of me.

I began my story just as the train jerked into motion,

and began to groan and grind its way out of the station. As it turned out, I didn't finish until the next morning. And I think I know why I confided in him as much as I did. It was because he listened so intently, seemed so riveted by every word I said. It was like I was telling my story to a little kid at bedtime. He just didn't want me to stop, and he kept asking questions, kept wanting me to explain things more. So it wasn't just me talking, it became more of a conversation between us than solo storytelling. And I had so much I wanted to show him, so much evidence: all the emails on the laptop, a typescript of Dad's story (rather battered by now) and Dad's copy of *The Ancient Mariner*, both of which I'd had with me on *Kitty Four* all the way from Australia. He loved the emails particularly, and he told me why too. It all became so real when he read them, he said, as if he was there on the boat with me.

So that's how I'll try to tell you my story then, just as I told it to Michael that first time, but without his interruptions.

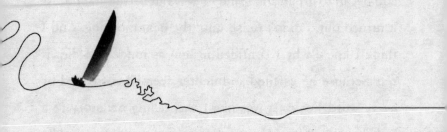

Two Send-offs, and an Albatross

Dad died just two weeks after I'd finally finished typing out his story. So he had his copy of it on his bedside table. He couldn't read it by this time, but he knew what it was all right, and he was very proud of it. The last time he was conscious I sang him his song over and over again, till I was sure he'd heard it. "London Bridge is falling down, falling down, falling down, London Bridge is falling down, my fair Lady."

He didn't open his eyes. But he squeezed my hand. He'd heard it.

We gave him a good Cretan send off, the kind he'd have liked, all of us there, the whole family, and we sang our songs and danced our dances. Then we went out in a flotilla of boats, Mum and me in *Kitty Four*, and we sprinkled his ashes far out at sea, just as he'd wanted us to do. I read a few verses from *The Ancient Mariner*. I knew his favourite lines, so I ended with them.

He prayeth well, who loveth well
Both man and bird and beast.

He prayeth best, who loveth best
All things both great and small;
For the dear God who loveth us,
He made and loveth all.

Just as I was finishing that last line an albatross came winging over us and floated above us on the air. Dad's spirit was in that bird. I knew it and so did Mum – we didn't have to say anything to know what the other was thinking.

As we watched it fly away I told her about the promise I'd made to Dad: that once he was gone, I'd do the voyage we were going to do together on my own. I'd sail to England, do all I could to find Kitty, and then sail home again. I expected an argument from her – I knew how nervous and upset she'd been about the whole project, and that was with two of us doing it. But she just said very quietly: "I know all about your promise, Allie. He told me, and besides I know his story, don't I? He was so proud of you. You go. You do it. It's what he would have wanted. But when it's done, you come back home, you hear?"

Fitting up *Kitty Four*, and planning the whole trip, and all the sea trials needed to test out the equipment, took several months. Mum wasn't going to let me go until she was quite sure everything on board was just as it should be. Grandpa was the same. He checked and double-checked everything. And all this time Mum was beginning the search for Kitty. She surfed the net, but that got her nowhere. She sent off emails to public record offices in London and all over England. Nothing. She wrote to one or two friends who lived there asking for their help. Everyone did what they could, but no one could find a trace of a Kitty Hobhouse born in London, probably in Bermondsey, at about the same time as Dad – though, like him, we could never be quite sure of when exactly that had been.

We set up a *Kitty Four* website so people could chart my progress at sea, and follow me all the way to England. And there was a link to the whole story of the search for Dad's missing sister asking anyone who might have any information about Kitty Hobhouse to get in touch. Maybe someone would read it. Hopefully someone would know something. We had hundreds of hits, huge interest, lots of good luck messages; but no one, it seems, had ever heard of a Kitty Hobhouse of Bermondsey, London.

Mum didn't give up. She and Grandpa used the press too. There were front-page articles in the newspapers, national as well as local. "Allie's Epic Voyage." "Allie Searches for Long Lost Auntie." I did radio interviews, TV interviews. Grandpa liked the TV coverage best of course because the boatyard's name was up there behind me: "Stavros Boats" in huge blue letters – bow to stern, the whole length of the boat, on my cap, on my wet weather gear, on just about everything. Grandpa was always there to stage the interview – he never missed a trick.

Mum thought the press coverage might be our best chance of tracking Kitty down. But no one phoned, no one got in touch, no one emailed. I got to thinking about what Dad had told me when he was a bit down once: that it had all been so long ago, that sometimes he wondered if Kitty had existed at all, that she could be just a figment of his imagination, that someone else could just as easily have given him his lucky key. So we could be looking for a figment.

As usual Mum stayed positive. Kitty was real, she was sure of it. Kitty was as real as her key, she said. She would keep looking while I was gone. Sooner or later, something had to turn up. All through Dad's illness she had been the same. Everyone around her only kept hoping because she did. Whatever made Dad feel better she made sure we did. Most of all he loved to see us dancing, all of us together, the whole family. "Let's do it like we always do it," she'd tell us, "so that he feels the joy in it." Even when he died, she was the strongest of us all. It was Mum's strength and determination that was to keep me going over the next five months. I could never have done it without her.

Mum was my coordinator back at home on shore through email, and through Satphone in an emergency. We would keep in touch every day. Any technical problems, I'd let her know. She'd talk to the blokes in the boatyard, and they'd do what they could to talk me through repairs and maintenance. Any injuries and health problems, she'd ask the doctor. We'd thought of everything, we hoped. We were as ready as we could be. All set to go. But I wasn't happy. There was a side to all this I was really beginning to dislike. Over the last weeks before I left I'd become a bit of a local celebrity, and I was finding the constant intrusion getting on my nerves. I just wanted to be gone. But I knew they'd be there, and lots of them, on the day I left. I wanted to slip away without anyone noticing, but Grandpa wasn't having any of it. He wanted me to have a proper send-off, a Cretan send off. The press was important, he said. He was proud of his little girl, proud of Stavros Boats, and he wanted the world to know it. And what Grandpa said, went. So that's how it happened.

I'd never seen so many cameras flashing in all my life. "This way, Allie." "Smile, Allie." I showed my teeth – it was all I could manage. But that apart, it was a send-off I'll never forget. The whole family turned out. Bouzoukis played on the jetty. They danced, they waved, they cried. Everyone from the boatyard was there, along with half of Hobart it seemed to me. All I wanted now was to be gone. I wanted the hugging and the tears to be over with. I just wanted to get on with it.

My first big worry was the dozens and dozens of motor boats and speedboats and jetskis and yachts that were escorting me down the Derwent River and out to the open sea. They were all around me, some of them very close, too close. Eyes in the back of my head would have been useful. I tried to wave them away, but they seemed to think I was waving goodbye to them and just waved back even more enthusiastically. But once we were past the Iron Pot and out in Storm Bay they all turned back, and I was on my own at last. We had a good breeze behind us and *Kitty Four* was sailing like a dream. I'd always loved *Kitty Four* – she'd been a dream for so long – but I never loved her more than I loved her now. She was going to be my home for five months. We'd be doing this together, just her and me, and Dad, who'd built her to sail the way she did, and made me the person I was, and the sailor I was too.

I sat there in the cockpit, the sun and the spray on my face, in seventh heaven – Dad was always counting heavens in his story, so I can too – singing *London Bridge is Falling Down* and drinking my first hot chocolate of the voyage. I was on my way.

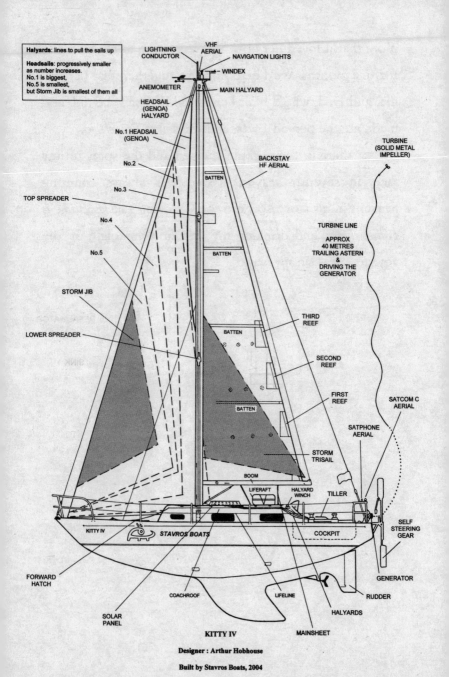

Halyards: lines to pull the sails up

Headsails: progressively smaller as number increases.
No.1 is biggest,
No.5 is smallest,
but Storm Jib is smallest of them all

LIGHTNING CONDUCTOR
VHF AERIAL
NAVIGATION LIGHTS
WINDEX
ANEMOMETER
MAIN HALYARD
HEADSAIL (GENOA) HALYARD
No.1 HEADSAIL (GENOA)
No.2
No.3
TOP SPREADER
No.4
No.5
STORM JIB
LOWER SPREADER
BACKSTAY HF AERIAL
BATTEN
TURBINE (SOLID METAL IMPELLER)
TURBINE LINE
APPROX 40 METRES TRAILING ASTERN & DRIVING THE GENERATOR
BATTEN
THIRD REEF
BATTEN
SECOND REEF
FIRST REEF
SATCOM C AERIAL
BATTEN
SATPHONE AERIAL
STORM TRISAIL
BOOM
LIFERAFT
HALYARD WINCH
TILLER
KITTY IV
STAVROS BOATS
COCKPIT
SELF STEERING GEAR
FORWARD HATCH
GENERATOR
COACHROOF
LIFELINE
RUDDER
SOLAR PANEL
HALYARDS
MAINSHEET

KITTY IV

Designer : Arthur Hobhouse

Built by Stavros Boats, 2004

KITTY IV
Below deck

HEADSAILS
(in bags)

ANCHORS

BIN

TOILET

PUMP

Shaded area – BUNK

DESALINATOR
(under bunk)

SINK

ICEBOX

STOVE

DRINKING
CHOCOLATE
STORE

ENGINE

Shaded area – COCKPIT
(but above deck)

SELF STEERING

TURBINE LINE

GENERATOR

PUMP

SEXTANT
(double wrapped
in plastic)

LAPTOP

NAVIGATION TABLE

HARNESS/LIFEJACKETS

Jelly Blobbers and Red Hot Chili Peppers

1600 hrs Mon 10 Jan 043' 23"S 148' 02"E

out past Tasman Island. great start. lumpy bumpy
sea. lumpy bumpy boat. nice of everyone to see me
off, except for that bloke in his jet ski who nearly
took my bow off he came so close. Anyways, he
missed, so still in one piece. Kept crying when I
looked back and saw you all waving, so that's why I
stopped waving after a while. wasn't being unfriendly
Grandpa. Every time I look up at the sails and see
Stavros Boats I'll think of you. And Mum every time I
use the laptop I'll be thinking of you. See you all in my
dreams too from time to time, that's if I get any
sleep which isn't likely.

Like I said to Mum I'll be writing emails whenever I can — you do the same, pleeeze — to let you know where I am, how I'm doing, how the boat's behaving, what the weather's doing.

I'm really loving this already, the emailing I mean. I talk a lot to myself anyway when I'm sailing because it's good to hear the sound of a voice, any voice, reassuring somehow, makes you feel there's someone else around — silly I know. So these'll be like talking emails. I sing a lot too, but I'll keep my singing to myself. You'll just have to imagine me up on deck belting out my Whitney Houston special in a force 8 or 9 — and ieeeiiieeei will always love you. I found myself humming London Bridge is Falling Down in the cockpit just now, like Dad did. I've got Dad's cds — louis armstrong, bob dylan, the beatles, buddy holly. I've got "What a Wonderful World" on right now, one of Dad's favourites when we were at sea together. Got my own stuff too — Coldplay, Red Hot Chili Peppers, few others. Couldn't take much, not enough room. piled high with junk down here, hardly any room for little old me. feel like a really big sardine in a really small can. Still it's home for a few months so I'd better get used to it. just hope the pc keeps going. lot depends on that. And that's down to the generator. Towing the turbine at 6 knots at present, so lots of amps. Amps = happy pc = happy me.

Just want to thank all of you for everything you did to get me this far. Kitty 4 is where she loves to be and so am I, and don't worry bout me too much. Got Dad's lucky key around my neck so I'll be fine.

Wind gusting 30 knots. Lots of jelly blobbers all around come to say goodbye too I spect. Saw my first albatross. Now I know Dad's out here with me, going all the way with me. See you.

2000hrs Tues 11 jan 44' 13"S 151' 12"E

Hi y'all. G'day. Settling in or trying to. Forgot how uncomfortable Kitty 4 really is. Didn't dear old Dad realise you've got to live in a boat as well as sail her?

Not enough room to swing a mouse down here. Sea kept me awake most of the night. Never shuts up, not for one moment. Banging and crashing all night, and if I got up never stopped chucking me about either. No consideration. I think she was just reminding me who's in charge out here. Gave up after a while and went up on deck, had some hot chocolate, yummy, and looked at the stars, zillions of them. Can't be any more beautiful place in the whole world than the sea at night when someone's switched on the stars. Hope heaven really is up there. Thought of Dad. Think of him often. Miss him, and when I miss him badly I talk to him. Tried to get some sleep again but I couldn't. Too keyed up. I still can't really believe I'm doing this, after all the years of building and planning, after everything that's happened. I lay there listening out for problems, for any strange creaks or groans. Kitty 4 talked to me all night, telling me she was fine, that I wasn't to worry. But once I start worrying I can't stop. S'not really worrying, it's just that my brain keeps churning things round and round and won't let me sleep.

Forecast was spot on. Wind from the north 50 knots. Funny how you forget things so quickly. You forget how busy you have to be. So much to be thinking about, so much to be doing and when it's done there's always something else. Which is why I've got to stop this and get some sail off.........

Back again. Read a bit of Dad's story again in the night, the beginning bit with him being sea-sick. I'm lucky. Don't do sea-sickness. Love reading his story because I can hear his voice in every word.

Kitty 4 sailing beautifully. Big rolling beam seas don't make it an easy ride, not for her, not for me. Still finding sea legs. Not hanging on hard enough, always banging my head. Big lump above my right ear. I'll hang on tighter next time. Huge tanker out there. Ugly great monster. Saw an albatross again, think it may be the same one. I tried to take a photo of him, but discovered the digital camera doesn't work. It did when I tried it out back home. I wanted to send pics on email, but now I can't. Very fed up. Sorreeee. Thanks for all the emails. Yes, Grandpa I am taking the vitamins. Hope I sleep better tonight. See soon. A.

1600 hrs Thurs 13 jan 45' 41"S 156' 19"E 5 knots

Love your emails. I love y'all. Miss y'all. I read them over and over. Yes Mum head's fine, no concussion. Yes Grandpa course I'll keep the Greek flag flying all the way, right up there with the Aussie one. Kitty 4 is a real beaut. Got y'all to thank for that, and Dad and Mr Dodds. She's a real marvel. Nothing I can teach her. She's teaching me. Got to be honest, it's a whole lot easier living alone on this boat. Dad was the best sailor in the world, but the untidiest. And he always hated me tidying up after him. He liked his own mess he said, knew where everything was. So I'd have to wait till he went up on deck then just tidy everything away quickly while he wasn't there. When he came back he'd never even notice I'd done it. Sound familiar Mum? He just loved living in a tip, that's all and I didn't. But give Dad his due, he was a brilliant cook (never washed up but he cooked like a dream).

He'd do all the cooking and let me sail the boat. All right so it was baked beans with everything. But he made the best bread, learned it off you Mum, the tastiest bread I ever tasted. Can't be bothered much with cooking at the moment. Just open a tin of something, anything, wolf it down then have my hot chocolate. That's what I live for, hot chocolate. I sit there all cold and wet and drink it down. It shivers the cold right out of me, warms me up from the inside up, reaches toeses and noses, all my freezing cold bits and pieces.

Decided this morning to learn The Ancient Mariner all the way through before I get to England. Think Dad would like that. Know the first verse already. Here it is. Not cheating, promise:

It is an ancient mariner
And he stoppeth one of three.
By thy long beard and glittering eye,
Now wherefore stopp'st thou me?

Up on deck earlier going along nice and easy, brilliant

sunshine. Saw the albatross again. It's the same one, sure of it now. He brought some of his friends with him to check me out. Seems to like me cos he stayed around for a while, they all did. He came so close I could see right into his eye and he could see into mine. I can't get it out of my head that maybe it's Dad keeping an eye out for me, doing this with me just as he always wanted to. When he flew off a few minutes ago I missed him, and the whole ocean seemed so empty and hostile too. I felt alone for the first time since I left.

Waves 10 metres and higher. Winds 30–40 knots all the time. Set the storm jib, not easy with the whole world pitching and rolling around me. Been up on deck doing too many sail changes, fifth today. Got to think ahead more. Got to limit the sail changes. Each one takes a lot out of me. When I get tired I make mistakes. Took the skin off my knuckles the last time I did it. Stupid. Little wounds don't heal out here easily. I've got two ginormous blisters already. Must look after them else they'll fester and festering isn't good, leads to all sort of nasties.

Wind patterns all over the place down here. Got to learn to predict the unpredictable, Allie – I can hear Dad saying it now. Doing my best, Dad. Halfway to Stewart Island, halfway to N.Z. Hot chocolate to celebrate. Listened to Coldplay. One or the other cheered me up – don't know which. Any news about Kitty, Mum? Be so so good if we could find her. Love you. A

And Now the Storm Blast Came

1700hrs Sat 15 Jan 46' 50"S 162' 49"E

Biggest storm last night, worst I've had. Gusts over 80 knots, waves 10 metres plus but the self-steering brought us through, easy as pie as Dad used to say. Can't say I enjoyed it much but Kitty 4 took it all in her stride. Made for it she is. Sat down below, wind howling all around and learnt another verse of the Ancient Mariner – can do the first eleven verses now without looking:

And now the STORM-BLAST came, and he
Was Tyrannous and strong:
He struck with his o'er taking wings
And chased us south along

Little strange and little funny to be sitting down here saying that over and over. I had to shout it out loud so I could hear myself. But it passed the time, kept me happy, made me think about something else besides the next towering wave out there. It was "Tyrannous and strong" all right. that Coleridge bloke knew what he was talking about.

Better now, heavy seas still but not anything like it was last night.

Averaging 5-8 knots, so that means we've done about 700 miles so far. Yippee! Hee hee!!! Well done Kitty 4 well done me! Good to know just how well Kitty 4 handles herself, feel she could cope with anything. I've always had confidence in her, but last night she really proved she could take it. She's so brave, so clever and I'm so lucky to be doing this with her. Lucky, lucky, lucky.

Lots of birds about today and best of all my albatross is here too. Just making sure we're all right after the storm, that's what I think. He really is the king of birds. He's got to have a wing span of 3 metres, massive, magnificent, MASSIFICENT, better word, my word. invented words are better words, mean more, say more. maybe that's the first time anyone has ever written that word. I like that, doing something for the first time, like going places no one's been before. At sea you do that all the time. I mean you sail up a wave and every one of them is unique, a new discovery, never seen before. You see clouds no one's seen before, and birds too. Course other sailors have seen albatross but not here not now not exactly the way I'm seeing mine. Difficult to put feelings into words but just want to say that's what's so great about being here cos it's like no one's ever been here before, that I've discovered it all for the first time. That's what it feels like anyway. Going on a bit. Sorry but I do love it, makes me feel so good, so lucky to be alive.

You should see my albatross. he doesn't fly, he doesn't need to. he just finds an airwave and floats — and you don't see his feet at all. They're tucked up neatly underneath him. There's hundreds of little birds all around him, recognised some storm petrels I think – Dad was better on birds than me, knew them all, knew so much. They dash about showing off, wing tips just not skimming the sea. And they're so fast, here, gone, swirling away. Wonderful.

Drying out after the storm, both of us, Kitty 4 and me. Soaked through, sodden. nowhere's dry, down in the cabin or up on deck. Not complaining, just dripping.

Reported sightings of icebergs little way south. got to be careful, really careful. icebergs worry me silly. So lots of cold sleepless nights ahead up there on watch. Wish the self-steering could do lookout as well. That's what I'll do one day, invent a self-steering system that does lookout as well. Easy. No problem. Make my fortune. Cool or what? Call it Stavros self-steering, all right Grandpa?

1641hrs Sun 16 Jan 2005

Sorry to hear about your cold Grandpa. You're always going on about me taking my vitamins and you go and get a cold. Stay in the warm. look after yourself. promise?

Fog now and rain, so got our lights on all the time. Icebergs don't see lights but other ships might. All you can do is listen and hope. Not too worried I tell myself cos there's a lot of water out here and very few ships. Still you think about it. It niggles at you all the time. Did a bit of fishing, but no luck. 82 miles now to the Snares south of Stewart Island. Cooked myself a great feast cos it's so miserable up there. No fish, so baked beans (of course) sausages and eggs and... and... and... wait for it two mugs of hot chocolate. Feel a lot better. Fog lifted a little so I could listen to Dad's Beatles CD, played his favourite song – here comes the sun – thought it might make the sun come out. Great song, but still no sign of sun up there. Read some of Dad's story. I love the parts when he was at his happiest, when Marty and Dad were living with Aunty Megs. Love the bit about that wombat "Henry's horrible hat hole", always makes me laugh.

No albatross today. Probably can't find us in the fog. Thought I saw a dolphin though v close to the boat. Can't be sure. Sea goes very quiet in fog. Even the waves seem to whisper. Can't spend too much time down below. Too risky. Got to keep an eye out. Got to keep listening. v. tiring. want to sleep. mustn't. got to go. Miss y'all. Think of you. Love you. A. P.S. Any news about Kitty?

1015hrs 17 Jan 41' 57"S 167' 31"E

Fog's lifted but feeling a bit low. Not enough sleep. All last night on watch and got to thinking about Dad again, I mean about him being here with me. Maybe it was reading his story that upset me, remembering all the sad things that happened to him. I shouldn't be sad because I know that he had good times too, specially during the best parts of his life, and with you and me Mum. But I just couldn't stop thinking about how much he wanted to be here doing this with me, that he made so much of this boat with his own hands. Maybe it's because I've always been so used to being on Kitty Four with him.

Maybe I was just imagining things, but I don't think so. I just felt he was there with me all night. I even thought I heard him humming London Bridge. I thought maybe telling you about it might help me make some sense of it. But it hasn't. Mum, I'm really beginning to believe he's still here with me on Kitty 4, like we really are doing this trip together just as we'd always planned we would. But there's something more. I need to believe it. I think the only way I'm going to get to England is to believe he's with me. at the same time I know I've got to stop feeling so sad about him, stop missing him so much. So I mustn't read his story again. I won't think of the past. Just focus on the here and now, it's the only way. Not going crazy, Mum, promise. We'll make it. Dad and me and Kitty 4. We'll make it. No worries. xxx A

1250hrs Tues 18 Jan 47' 31"S 170' 36"E

Hi Mum hi Grandpa. Feeling a whole lot better. Not sad any more. Slept really well. Didn't want to get up at all. Always the same. Tell you why.

1. You don't want to get up there and get wet again soon as you stick your nose out up top.

2. Socks. You can always smell where they are and you don't want to go near them ever again.

3. Boots always waiting for you where you left them. Step right in, they say, and it'll be lovely and wet and cold, hee hee.

But once you're in your boots, in your wet weather gear which is always still wet, it doesn't seem to matter any more. It's done. I make a nice hot chocolate to warm myself through. Then suddenly I'm up there in the cockpit out of the stench of socks and diesel and damp, and the ocean is heaving all around, and it's the best place in the whole world to be. And this morning, guess what, my albatross was back. He was there waiting for me. And... And... And... he's brought dolphins with him, dozens of them dancing all around me. Never been so happy in my life. What was it you called me once, Mum? Moody? Moi? OK you were right. Waves go up and down — why shouldn't I?? Even my blisters are all better. Love you lots. Allie

Just Staying Alive

1830hrs Sat 22 Jan

DUNEDIN NZ!

Hi Mum, hi Grandpa. Sorree. Sorree, sorry you
haven't heard much from me for a while. Been a bit
busy just staying alive. Can't say I wasn't warned.
Grib weather forecasts were the worst ever, so I knew
it was coming. Trouble was I couldn't get out of the
way of it. Ellen MacArthur would have been able to go
round it, dodge it, or race ahead of it. She can do
fast, I can't. Kitty 4 doesn't do fast. But she does
do brave. And it wasn't just grib that warned me, my
albatross did too. Not kidding. For two whole days

before the storm he never left us. He was telling us, I'm sure he was. He just hung there above us looking down on us. He'd never stayed so close before nor for so long.

The storm came suddenly, 50–60 in squalls and huge blue waves so high you didn't want to look but you had to. And blue so deep you could see right into it. Just before it happened I was doing a sail change and clipped on, thank goodness. You know how you can feel thunder is about before you hear it, like the sky is taking a deep breath before it lets rip. It was like that. There was a strange silence and a stillness all around. Like the sea was waiting for it to happen. Then I looked up and saw this wall of water 15 metres high at least and it was breaking right over me, and my albatross was skimming along the crest of it like he was telling me to hang on. So I hung on. Kitty 4 was knocked down, rolled through 140 degrees. The mast was under the water. I thought that was it, that she'd just go on rolling and turn turtle and that would be that. End of story, I thought. But it wasn't the end of the story. She lay there on her side for a few moments like she was having a bit of a rest and then she just flipped right back up again, a bit like Kitty in my bath back home when I was little. Everything was crashing about. I was chucked about like a wet rag doll. Not a single bit of me that wasn't bruised. But no broken bones, and what's a bruise or two when you're still alive.

And that was just the beginning. Went on for nearly thirty hours. By the time it was over Kitty 4 had taken a real battering — she was in a much worse state than me which is why Mum, Grandpa, I'm here in Dunedin. Had to put in for repairs. The light fitting on the mast head needs draining for a start. Needed a new set of steering lines cos they had chafed badly. Can't do without my self-steering gizmo. It's my magic pathfinder through the waves, like my best friend. Got to look after him. And there's a mainsail that's torn, so that needed fixing too. In a way I'm glad I got knocked down, glad I had to come into Dunedin. Taught me a lesson. Been a chance to reorganise, tie everything down properly that flew around. thought I'd done that already but the storm found me out. Won't be my last knockdown on this trip. Be better set up next time.

And anyway I needed to do some shopping too, more plasters and antiseptic cream. baked beans and hot chocolate supplies were low. Everyone v. kind here in Dunedin, v. helpful. Lots of press people came to see me so lots of posing by Kitty 4. Maybe you saw some of it. Don't worry Grandpa I made sure I had my Stavros Boats cap on. you're going to be selling loads of boats in Dunedin after this, all over NZ. And guess what I've got free bed and breakfast for all the time I'm here — gift from the town. Isn't that the best?

2015hrs same day

Just spoken to you on the phone. So good to hear your voices. Made me cry though. And like I said Mum don't worry, I promise I wouldn't be going on with this if I thought the boat wasn't up to it. She's fine. She won't get there in a hurry, but she'll get there, bobbing all the way. Best bobbing boat in the world. I'm fine. Like I told you the bruises don't hurt like they did. pretty dramatic to look at though. got one all the colours of the rainbow right across my ribs. spectacular. Been having lots of sleep in my nice warm bed and I've had lots of long hot baths. I'm taking on all the warmth I can. Like a camel taking on water before a journey across the desert, I'm going to need it, I know that. Told you most of my news on the phone, but must tell you about my albatross.

Saw him last night, but only in my dreams. Dreamt of Dad too. Can't remember all that much of it, never can remember my dreams properly, but I think I remember Dad and the albatross seemed to be one and the same somehow. One or the other of them, and I don't know which, was singing London Bridge is Falling Down. Weird or what?

All being well should be on our way again soon. Weather pattern looking better, so that's good. Bout time. I want some nice easy sailing. Oh yes, and I can do up to verse 20 of the Ancient Mariner by heart now. v pleased with myself! Been learning a couple of verses a day in the bath since I've been here. Don't think I understood till now why Dad loved it so much. I just lie there soaking in my bath saying the lines over and over:

God save thee ancient Mariner!
From the fiends that plague thee thus!
Why look'st thou so? – with my crossbow
I shot the ALBATROSS

That's verse 20. Sad but so beautiful. I'll know it all word perfect by the time I get to England. Promise. A

P.S. Still no news of Kitty? Keep thinking and hoping no news will soon be good news.

1002hrs Sat 29 Jan 48' 12"S 173' 45"E

6 knots. heading south in brilliant sunshine, reef in the mainsail. The mend is holding well which is good news. It's all good news because my albatross is

back. It's like he's been waiting for me out here all the time I was in Dunedin. Seen plenty of them about, but they just fly by on their way to somewhere else. He's the only one who hangs about. He's like my guardian angel. So I've got Dad's lucky key and I've got a guardian angel too. I'm well looked after Mum. I keep throwing him some scraps because I really want him to stay. The trouble is that as soon as I throw him food his friends come back and bully him off it. I've decided to do some more fishing from now on – never did it with Dad, he didn't like it. It's too easy just to open a tin. Besides I love fish, full of protein and good for me. Keeps me strong. Don't like the idea of killing them, but do like eating them. So I'm going to keep a line out and baited whenever I can. I'll get lucky sooner or later.

1122hrs Sun 30 Jan 49' 02"S 175' 38"E

More fog. Can't see a thing, except a bit of sea around us and my albatross. flies in and out of the fog like a ghost, a welcome ghost though. Doing less than 2 knots, not even enough to charge the battery with the turbine and there's not enough sun for the solar panel to be much use either. need a minimum of 4 knots to keep going and that's with everything off except the laptop and the instruments. Can't afford to use diesel to motor out of it. Can't afford to use laptop any more either. So I'm turning you off. Byeee Mum. Bye Grandpa. A

0735hrs Wed 2 Feb 49' 52"S 173' 54"E

756 miles since Dunedin. Antipodes islands behind us. The Horn ahead of us. Long way to go still. Not worrying about it, Mum, just thinking about it, getting myself ready. Desalinator not working as well as it should. Water tastes a bit salty. But otherwise no worries. Clothes a bit smelly. Glad it's only me on Kitty 4. Must have a big wash soon, me and my clothes. Been putting it off.

Doing 7 knots sometimes, averaging 4.5. So I'm doing well. I thought my albatross had deserted me yesterday but he hasn't. He's up there now, helping us along putting wind in our sails with his great wide wings. He just comes and goes as he pleases. I feel adopted. Out of all the ships and boats in the Southern Ocean I feel he's chosen us. He likes me to sing to him too, always seems to come closer when I do. So I've done him my Whitney Houston, all the Beatles songs I know — Dad taught me most of them — and when I run out I whistle him "London Bridge is Falling Down". He seems to like that best. Still no fish, but I'll keep trying. There's got to be millions of fish down there, all of them deliberately ignoring my line. Why is that? What have they got against me? My smelly clothes? My singing? Thought I saw the back of a whale yesterday. Too big for a dolphin. Got all excited, but if he was one he didn't show himself again. Hope he doesn't have a nibble at my bait. Not really the kind of fish I'm after. Bit big. This is how sailing should be. We're dancing our way towards the Horn.

I'm having big doubts about Kitty, like Dad had. Maybe he did make her up after all. I really want to believe he didn't. I've been trying to keep my hopes up, but it's difficult. To go all the way to England and find out there's no Kitty after all would be so sad, for Dad and for me. Think positive. Must believe the best. When I do that I get to thinking about what I'm going to say to Kitty when we meet. I can't wait to see the look on her face when I tell her who I am. And to have a relation on Dad's side too would be really something. Got so many on your side – no offence Grandpa. But we need some balance here. I'm only half Greek y'know. And I know you don't want to hear this but I've always liked cheddar cheese beta than feta! Now you know and you'll hate me forever. S'agapo, I love you, Grandpa. xxx A

"Hey Ho Little Fish Don't Cry, Don't Cry"

Dad used to love old black and white Spencer Tracey movies, any Spencer Tracey movie. If it was on we watched it. And one film in particular he loved. It was called *Captains Courageous*. Tracey plays this old fisherman on a whaling ship. He looks after a young boy who's very spoilt and teaches him what's what, right from wrong, fair from unfair. He sings him an old fishing song, and I loved this song. It was one of those songs that just stayed in my head. I used to sing it all the time, out on the boat with Dad, in the bath at home, wherever I was happy. And now here I was in the Southern Ocean on my way to the Horn on *Kitty Four* catching and killing my first fish (I've never liked that part of it), tears pouring down my cheeks and singing out Spencer Tracey's fishing song:

"Hey ho little Fish, don't cry, don't cry. Hey ho little Fish don't cry."

That first one I couldn't bring myself to eat, so I tossed it overboard for my albatross who had been watching me, probably hoping I'd do just that. He didn't have to be asked twice. He was in the sea in a flash and swallowed it down. He didn't actually lick his lips, but he looked pretty pleased as he sat there in the sea waiting for more. When I caught my next fish, I ate it myself, despite lots of hurt looks from my albatross. But I did chuck him the head, which he gobbled down more than happily.

Whenever I caught a fish after that my albatross seemed to be waiting, so I always threw him the head. I got less squeamish about boning and gutting them too, and I learned how to cook them better each time. The truth is that I began to enjoy the whole process, from the excitement of seeing the line go taut to the eating itself. So now unless it was really stormy I'd have a line out astern of me most of the time.

Routine was all important to living on *Kitty Four*. It kept my spirits up. Routine checks of everything up on deck – regular adjustments to the halyards and the steering lines. Regular meals and hot meals too, if the weather allowed. The weather rules everything at sea, so sailing the boat came first. But I tried to live as normal a life as possible, tried not to allow the sea to dictate how I spent every moment of my day. So I learned my *Ancient Mariner*. I wrote my emails. I tidied the cabin. I played my CDs. I mended what had to be mended – there was always something. I fitted the spare membrane to my troublesome desalinator, superglued what had to be superglued. I washed clothes, not as often as I should, and hung them out to dry. I liked to keep myself clean too – to begin with I hadn't cared about it, but the longer I was at sea the more important it became. So I washed whenever I could – I always felt so much better for having made the effort. And on fine nights, however hard it was blowing, I'd always do the same thing. I'd go up into the cockpit if possible with my cup of hot chocolate and I'd watch the stars. I'd do a lot of my singing up there too – everything from *London Bridge* to *Hey ho Little Fish* to *Yellow Submarine*.

It was on just such a night that I first saw it. I was sitting there gazing up at the zillions of stars, wondering if Grandpa back home was also sitting there with his telescope doing the very same thing at the very same moment, remembering how he loved to tell me what each of them was called, how he'd help me to hold his telescope myself. I was remembering all this when I saw a shooting star pass overhead, much lower and brighter and slower than shooting stars usually were. I watched in amazement as this light arced across the sky, knowing already it couldn't be a shooting star. It had to be a satellite of some kind. I went down below at once and emailed home to see if Grandpa knew what it could be. Until now I'd never had an email direct from Grandpa – they had always come through Mum. But the next day he emailed me back himself. "I checked. Got to be the ISS. International Space Station."

I saw it up there again a few nights later even brighter this time, even closer, and I got to thinking: those astronauts up there are closer to me at this moment than any other human being on earth. I'm sailing the seas down here. They're sailing through space up there. I wondered then if with all their high-tech gizmos they could see me. I felt like waving. So I stood there in the cockpit and waved and shouted till my arms ached, till my throat was sore. I was just so excited, so so happy to see them up there. That was when the idea first came to me to try to make contact with them, proper contact. Wouldn't it be wonderful, I thought, to meet up by email or even by phone, so we could actually talk to one another as they passed over? I sent an email to Grandpa. It was just a crazy idea to start with, just a lovely dream. Grandpa emailed back. "No worries. I'll fix it." I thought he was joking. Meanwhile I had a boat to sail.

I was still about 1000 miles from the Horn. I was down to 57°S. There was ice about in the south, lots of it. It was cold you couldn't forget, the kind that got into your bones, deep into your kidneys. Feet and hands went numb, so when I cut myself, and I often did, I couldn't feel it. My ears and my nose ached with it. I used to warm my socks and gloves on the kettle, but the trouble was that my toes and fingers were always colder than my socks and gloves were warm. So the bliss never lasted for long. I'd never known cold like it. I'd do all I could to stay down below in the warm fug I'd created for myself. But sooner or later I'd always have to go back up there again, and the snugger I'd make myself, the colder the blast that hit me when I got up into the cockpit.

It was too rough for fishing now, and far too cold anyway, but my albatross was usually still there. He'd go off for a day or two, but I knew he'd always come back, and he did. I had such faith in him, that he'd stay with me and see me safely round the Horn. And I knew why too, knew it for sure, though I'd stopped writing about it in my emails because I thought it might upset Mum, and because I know it sounded at best a bit crazy. But I knew I wasn't hallucinating, that I wasn't mad. I now knew for sure that it was Dad's spirit soaring up above *Kitty Four*. He was an albatross, of course he was, but he was Dad too.

It was a different world I was sailing in down there, the wildest place I'd ever been. I could see and feel the swell building all the time. South of 60° between Cape Horn and the Antarctic peninsula there's no land to break up the ocean swells, so the waves travel uninterrupted for hundreds of miles and they're just massive – I kept using the word "awesome" in my emails, and that was about right. I knew *Kitty Four* could handle them, but I also knew I couldn't leave it all to her. I had to be out there avoiding the breaking waves, especially the hollow ones, the ones that look as if they're going to swallow you up. Sleep was almost impossible in seas like this, in weather like this. The wind screamed all the time. It was a constant pounding. I was on edge, listening to the boat, trying to work out if she was just complaining, or whether she was telling me something was really wrong. Like me, she was finding this very hard. We were both being tested as never before.

Below in the cabin was my whole world for hours on end. It was cramped, but down there I felt warm and safe. My bunk was a tight fit – it had to be because falling out was very painful and dangerous too. But it wasn't comfortable. I'd lie there surrounded by all the stuff that was keeping me alive – the medical box, generator, stove, charts, almanacs, sextant, pc, spares for everything, harnesses, life vests and sails – and kept telling myself that

Kitty Four and all this equipment would get me through. And when I went up on deck there was my albatross telling me exactly the same thing. It was scary, it was heart-thumpingly scary at times, but I never for one moment thought we wouldn't make it. And whenever I felt like human company, I'd sing to myself or listen to a CD, or email home. In my emails I tried to hide just how scary it really was sometimes. There was no point in upsetting Mum and Grandpa unnecessarily. Tell them some of it, I thought, but there's no need to tell them everything.

I was finding the keyboard slow to use now because my fingers were becoming very swollen. I couldn't feel them, and they looked like a bunch of white bananas. I was doing all I could to look after them, smothering them with lanolin, but still the cracks came, still my cuticles split around my nails – what nails I had left. My hands were not a pretty sight, but I didn't mind. I just wanted them to work, to be able to do what I told them to do – cook, tie knots, pull ropes, email.

I've never forgotten the morning I saw Cape Horn up there on the laptop screen at last. Sometime before I left home I'd seen the movie *Master and Commander*, seen the frigate battling its way through ferocious seas off the Horn. It was terrifying enough sitting in a comfy seat next to Dad in the cinema in Hobart. Soon now I'd be going round the Horn myself, doing it for real, but Dad was still beside me. He was there in the boat he'd made for us, in the albatross that guarded us, and in my heart too. I took out *The Ancient Mariner* which by now had become like a Bible to me. It gave me new determination, a new courage every time I read it out loud.

The ice was here, the ice was there,
The ice was all around:
It cracked and growled, and roared and howled,
Like noises in a swound!

At length did come an Albatross,
Thorough the fog it came;
As if it had been a Christian soul,
We hailed it in God's name.

Every time I spoke those words now, I felt that somehow I was living inside the poem, that it had been written just for Dad and me, just for this moment as we approached the Horn on the 9th March.

Around the Horn, and with Dolphins Too!

2005hrs 9 Mar 55' 47"S 74' 06"W

Dear Mum, dear Grandpa, dear everyone. Feels like this really is the bottom of the earth down here. The sky up there is black with rain squalls and the wind's screaming like I've never heard it before. this is not a funny place to be. don't think I'll hang about. Kitty 4 doesn't seem to care though. she just bounces along, two storm jibs up twin poled, 6 knots, riding each wave like it was just a ripple. If this was a talking boat – bout the only thing she can't do! –

she'd be shouting at the waves — bring it on baby, gimme more, see if I care, you think you can beat me? no way hosay! And you should see the waves she'd be shouting at. Bout 15 metres from bottom to top, so when you're down in a trough and look up they look as if they're about 50 metres. And they're long, that's what makes them different. They've travelled all around the world just to meet us here — aren't they nice? aren't they kind? — building all the time. Up to 200 metres long, I promise you. Awesome, magnificent, majestic, amazing, exhilarating, overwhelming (running out of adjectives so I'll stop). They're wave monsters that's what they are, and when one decides to break it's like an avalanche that goes on and on, and Kitty 4 does snowboarding then surfing through the middle of it, raging white water all around, the air snowing foam. So beautiful, so wonderful. Should be scary but it's not. Too excited to be frightened, too much to think about, too much to do. And maybe I'm too Cretan to be scared, Grandpa!

And besides, I keep thinking that every wave brings

us nearer to the Horn. The Horn is dead ahead by my reckoning, only 230 miles to go — can you believe that? We should be going around it on Friday if all goes well. It's strange, I'm not worried at all. Maybe that's because my albatross is still up there, still with us. He hovers over the bow, like he's leading us, like he's showing us the way. Wind doesn't seem to bother him at all. I mean why isn't he just blown away? How does he do it? He looks like he's playing with the wind, like he's having fun with it, teasing it. He's not just the king of the birds, he's the master of the wind too. Against the black of the clouds he looks whiter than he's ever been, white as an angel, a guardian angel. I keep saying it I know, but that's what he looks like to me. Had the last of my sausages and baked beans for my supper. Got to go easy on the hot chocolate. run out if I'm not careful. One little problem, caught my little finger in a rope, think it's broken so I've strapped it up. can't feel it most of the time so that's good. I can hear what you're saying Mum. Yes, I'll be careful. Got 9 more fingers. So no worries. Loving this. Love you. Allie.

1825hrs 11 Mar 56' 00"S 67' 15"W

Done it done it done it! Woweee! We're going around the Horn and with dolphins too, and my albatross of course. I'm going to tell you how it was. I knew the Horn was there, but I couldn't see her. Every time we climbed a wave in the last four hours I was looking for her, but she was never there. So from time to time, I'd go down to check the screen. The Horn was always on the screen but never where she should be when I went back up into the cockpit again. It was so so frustrating. Kitty 4 didn't seem to want to stay on the top of a wave long enough for me to catch my first glimpse of land. Then I did. I whooped and yelled and sang and danced, well sort of, not a lot of room for dancing in the cockpit. And my albatross swooped down low over the boat almost touching me as he flew by. Then he soared up high and went off towards the Horn, to have a look I guess. He'll be back.

I've been dreaming about this moment, Mum, Grandpa, ever since I first read about it, or did Dad talk about it first, can't remember. And now I'm doing it. I'm here. Kitty 4 is poled out, full main. No squalls about. West wind 15-20 knots. Got to change the flags soon, Chilean to Argentinian. Aussie and Greek one still up there Grandpa, looking a bit battered and torn, like me. But they're still flapping away up there, like they're really happy, really proud we've made it. Me too, me too. I'm flapping with happiness.

The rocks of the Horn do not look at all inviting — wouldn't want to be any closer, black and jagged when you can see them through the sea mist. grey and grim and dismal. been so lucky with the weather. Not hard to imagine what this place can be like in a Force 10 when it's really angry. Underneath us, the seabed must be littered with all those ships who didn't make it, those who didn't get so lucky. I thought a lot about that when I was sitting there half an hour or so ago, drinking a celebratory hot chocolate — who needs champagne when you've got hot chocolate?

I think I just had a moment I'll never forget. I so wished you were with me, and Dad most of all. I was just sitting there looking at the Horn and sipping the last of my hot chocolate when a shaft of evening sunlight broke through the mist and lit the Horn. It set her on fire and all the sea around her too. Never in my life saw anything so beautiful. Don't mind telling you, I had a little weep. It was the joy of just being here at this moment, of being alive, grateful to y'all, to the Horn for letting us sail by, to my albatross for sticking with us, to dear old Dad who's made it all happen and who's been with me all through this and is here with me now.

I love this place so much I almost don't want to leave it, don't want the moment to pass. But moments always pass, don't they? It's passed even as I was writing this. Gone. I'd better be gone too.

I'll be going up north towards the Lion Islands, just south of the Falklands, a little over 300 miles away. Stop in the Falklands for a few days, have lots of long hot baths – been dreaming of those – and lots of big breakfasts and a warm dry bed for a few nights. Been a bit lax on my washing lately – blame it on the weather – whole plastic bags of it waiting. one whiff would kill, promise. So I'll get all my washing done. Be so good not to be rocking and rolling every hour of every day, not to be banging my head all the time. Be good to see people again. Be good to be dry. And yes Mum I'll do what you say and get my little finger checked out.

Went up into the cockpit a few minutes ago and my albatross is back from the Horn, done his explorations. He's sitting in the sea, and by the look in his eye he'd like another fish. Soon as we turn north I'll put the line out again, and hope to catch a fish or two. That should keep him happy. It should be flatter that side, so better for fishing. Then up to the Falklands for a bit of a rest. I need it. Kitty 4 needs it. she needs a good clean – covered in barnacles and slime. Slimy she may be but she's done Hobart to the Horn in 60 days. Not another boat like her in the whole world. Just gave her a smacking great kiss to tell her I loved her. Put Louis Armstrong on the CD. "What a Wonderful World". It is too.

2115 same day

Just got all your congrats, thank you, thank you, and and and and your grate grate news Mum about Kitty, you said something would turn up and it has, but only because you never gave up. Love you so much. It's incredible, brilliant, wonderful, grate! So I've got a whole new family I never knew about! And Kitty is real, really real, not a figment of Dad's imagination. Tell that bloke who emailed you that he's the best vicar in the entire world. When I get to England I'm going to go to St James in Bermondsey to see the baptism records for myself, see the place where they were baptised. I keep looking at the family tree you sent me, Mum, I can't believe it! New grandparents! Ellen and Sidney Hobhouse. And the marriage certificate too – Ellen Barker (spinster) Sidney Hobhouse (cobbler). Now I know for sure that Dad was a baby once! He was a happening, wasn't he?!! And so was Kitty. Like you say Mum we mustn't get our hopes up too much. We still have to find Kitty, and when we do it may be too late, she could be dead, but at least we know she is or was a true person, a happening, just like Dad, real just like Dad. Will you thank the vicar bloke from me too for helping us like this and tell him I want to meet him when I come to London. So Dad was right about Bermondsey too. Is that far from London Bridge? He had a better memory than he thought he had, dear old Dad, didn't he? Best day of my life, I've rounded the Horn and I've found a new family. This calls for another hot chocolate, maybe two. Know I shouldn't, know I'll run out. But who cares? A

xxxxxxxxxxxxxxxxxxxxxxxxxxx – zillions of them.

Dr Marc Topolski

Thinking back I should have stayed longer in the Falkland Islands. I didn't, mostly because the hopeful news I'd just had about Kitty made me impatient to be on my way again. The Falklands is a bleak and barren place, that's for sure, and the people are tough – they have to be. But they were kindness itself. My arrival caused quite a stir. Lots of people were following my trip now on the website, so they knew I was coming. I had lots of helping hands, and a place to stay in Stanley which was a home from home for me. Mrs Betts mothered me like a happy hen who has just found a lost chick. I had all the baths I'd been longing for, all the breakfasts too. I did a couple of interviews, but then she made sure I was left alone to recover.

And *Kitty Four* was well looked after too. Within a week she was tidy and trim again, not a trace of slime, and the barnacles gone. She was ready to go. The solar panel was fixed – I'd been having a lot of trouble with that. She was filled up with diesel, and I had all the provisions on board I needed to get me to England, all the packets of hot chocolate I could ever want! I was just waiting for the right wind, and the right tide. But an onshore wind was blowing a gale, and it went on blowing for days on end, apparently quite common in the Falklands. So I couldn't leave. If I'd tried I would have been crunched against the jetty.

Mrs Betts offered to show me the island a bit while I was waiting. So off we went in her little Morris Minor van, bumping our way across the island. She took me all over, told me about the daughter she had who'd left the island and was living in New Zealand and had a baby now, but how she'd never seen her grandchild. I told her a bit about Dad. She knew something about him already from the newspapers, and she made me recite *The Ancient Mariner* just to prove to her that I could – she'd heard about that too, from the website I guessed. I knew almost forty verses by then, so she got the lot. We saw penguins and we saw sheep, all huddling against the cold of the wind. She took me to the British war cemetery, and told me about the war they'd had there when the Argentinians invaded the island twenty years before. It made me so sad to see all those graves. Standing there, the wind whipping about us, I thought of Dad and Vietnam, of young men dying a long way from home. "They were fine boys," Mrs Betts said suddenly. "But then so were the Argentinians. And they all had mothers."

That evening, my last on the Falklands, I read her the last part of *The Ancient Mariner*, because she said she wanted to know what happened. She had tears in her eyes when I'd finished. "So in a way it's a kind of happy ending," she said. Then she looked at me hard. "I'll be thinking a lot about you, Allie. I want your journey to have a happy ending too. And I want you to find Kitty. You deserve a happy ending."

She offered me her phone then to ring home. She said I should, that a daughter needs to speak to her mother, that emails weren't enough. So for ten minutes I talked to Mum and Grandpa, who kept snatching the phone from one another. We laughed a lot and cried a lot too, which meant we didn't say as much as we should have. Grandpa kept going on about a "big surprise" that he couldn't tell me about yet, and then he would almost tell me, and Mum would snatch the phone off him again, and I could hear her telling him off, that he'd promised to say nothing, not until they could be sure of it. I was certain I knew what it was.

"You've found Kitty, haven't you?"

"No, it's not that," Mum said. "But we're still looking."

"Then what's the surprise?" I asked.

"Nothing, nothing," she told me. But I knew something was going on.

I had a big send-off the next day, and as we said goodbye Mrs Betts gave me a digital camera. "A going away present, because yours doesn't work, dear," she said. "This one does, I promise."

And so it did too. The first photo I took was of Mrs Betts waving goodbye from the jetty. I was in such high spirits. I was on *Kitty Four* again. I'd had all my home comforts with Mrs Betts – but I'd missed *Kitty Four*, missed the smell of her, missed the movement of the sea underneath me. This was my real home. This was where I wanted to be. I knew I had a lot of tomorrows ahead of me before I reached England, about sixty-five days away. Then I'd go to London, go to St James in Bermondsey, and find Kitty if I could. As I left the Falklands, I had never felt better about the outcome of the whole expedition.

But now I was back at sea I had one growing doubt, and it was a doubt that nagged me every hour of every day that followed. My albatross wasn't there. I had dolphins, dozens of them all around me. But the last I'd seen of my albatross was the day we'd sailed into the Falklands. I'd just presumed that he'd be out there, that he'd be just waiting for us to put to sea again.

I was wrong. The days went by. I began to feel so alone without him. My emails became shorter and shorter at this time, partly because I didn't want Mum to know how miserable I was, and partly because I wanted to be up there in the cockpit as much as possible so that I would be there when he came. But he didn't come and he didn't come. And by now I'd worked out why of course. Albatross rarely come this far north. They are southern ocean birds, I knew that. But I went on hoping he'd come back anyway. I tried to keep myself as busy as I could, tried so hard not to dwell on my loneliness. But I couldn't sleep at nights now for thinking about my albatross. I was beginning to believe, in the darkness of those long nights, that I really was on my own now, that Dad had gone too, gone with the albatross. I had been right about that then: they were one and the same. Having been so hopeful, so sure of everything, I was suddenly overwhelmed with misery.

There was a lot of kelp about, ugly-looking stuff, the bubbly kind, the thistly kind, and some of it in very thick long strands of up to twenty metres. And it was all around the boat. I felt hemmed in by it, threatened. It looked like writhing sea snakes coming to get me, reaching out to grab me. It would rise up on either side as we ploughed through it. I longed not to have to look at it, to go below, but I couldn't. It wasn't just because I was looking for my albatross that I needed to be up on deck. I had other reasons.

There were suddenly a lot of fishing boats around down there, I could see them easier at night all along the horizon – and fishing boats were every bit as dangerous as icebergs. Get caught in the miles of nets they trail behind them and I knew that would be the end of everything. I hadn't ever felt this low before. To make it worse my pc was playing up, and for the first time on the trip I could neither send nor receive. The wind died. The sea stilled. There was grey sea, grey sky all around, and I was marooned in a sea of serpents. I sang to keep my spirits up. I could think of nothing else to do. I sang till my throat ached, every song I'd ever known. But one song I sang again and again, *London Bridge is Falling Down*. It was a cry of pain, I think, but also a cry for help.

How fast things can change at sea. I came up into the cockpit one morning to find the kelp all gone, the fishing boats nowhere to be seen. And the wind was up and gusting. It was like the whole earth had suddenly woken up around me. Where there had been grey, there was blue, endless blue, beautiful blue. I breathed in deep and closed my eyes. When I opened them, he was there floating down towards me on the wind. An albatross, my albatross. He didn't care about north or south. He just wanted to come with me. When I'd finished all my crying and whooping I told him exactly what I thought of him leaving me in the lurch like that for so long. Albatross can't smile of course, that's what most people think. But they can and they do. They smile all the time. And when I threw him a fish I'd caught for him that evening he was smiling all right. I know he was.

I was down below in the cabin a couple of hours later, baking the first bread I'd made since leaving the Falklands, and still revelling in the memory of my reunion with the albatross. His return had not only cheered me, it had clearly had some magical effect on my pc which was now working again, perfectly. Then the phone rang, the Satphone. It had rung only a few times on the whole trip, and then it had always been a coastguard calling, and always much nearer land. I picked it up, worried there might be something wrong at home, or maybe it was just Mum panicking because she hadn't been able to reach me on email.

"Hi there," it was a man's voice. "This is Dr Marc Topolski. You don't know me" – he had an American accent – "but your Grandpa's been speaking with NASA. They phoned right up and suggested I might like to talk with you."

I didn't understand what he was on about, not at first. "I'm not ill," I said. "I don't need a doctor. I'm fine."

"Sure you are, Allie. Thing is, Allie, that I'm up here right above you in the International Space Station, and you're right down below us, and your Grandpa said you can see us sometimes and how you'd like to get in touch. And I thought that seemed like a fine idea, because we're both kind of explorers, aren't we? And so I thought like you did, that maybe we could like get together on email or by phone, from time to time, whatever you like, a kind of ongoing conversation. Might be fun. Might be interesting. What do you say?"

I couldn't say a thing.

I had that first amazing phone call from space, so my emails tell me, on the 29th March. Grandpa's surprise was a surprise all right, the surprise of my life.

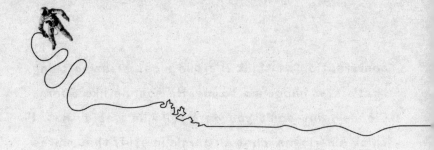

"One Small Step for Man"

0715hrs 29 March 45' 44"S 50' 13"W

G'day best Grandpa in the world. No question. You are the coolest Grandpa that ever lived, the greatest, the greekest. Just had the surprise you told me about, the one you made happen. I can't imagine anything more surprising happening to anyone ever anywhere. Thank you, thank you Grandpa. He's going to send me a pic of himself and the crew up there, and we're going to have what he calls "an ongoing conversation". I think it's the most amazing thing that's ever happened to me. He sounds like George Clooney, but don't you dare tell him I said that. I think Americans must all gargle in stuff that makes their voices so husky. And... and... and, what you don't know is that my albatross is back with me too! So I got an albatross and an astronaut all in one day. Not bad eh? Don't know how long my albatross can stay. He's already way too far north. I'm going to try to feed him lots of fish to keep him with me, which is silly I know because he can catch all the fish he wants for himself, albatross are quite good at that stuff, but he seems to like hanging around for mine too. Can't believe how many of you are looking out for me now out here, all of you at home, my albatross and now Dr Topolski. No one ever had a supporters' club like that before. Grib forecast is horrible, so I've got lots to do and in a hurry. I'll get back to you later soon as I can. Love y'all, specially you greek Grandpa. Axx

1112 hrs 31 March 42' 29"S 48' 30"W

Hi Mum, g'day Grandpa, not had a lot of time to do anything except sail the boat. So have had no time to write emails to you or to Dr Topolski. Just been through a storm like no other. Two knockdowns, but I'm still alive and kicking, still here to tell the tale so no worries. Most of the time there was nothing to do but hunker down below and hope, getting quite good at that. did a lot of bad singing and quite a lot of clutching Dad's lucky key too. 70 knot gusts rising to 80. vicious wind. Massive flat top waves, wind flattened, the worst kind, the really dangerous kind. Breaking waves of grey water, a spray storm all around me. I just tried to keep the wind and the swell on the quarter as much as I could. Not always possible which is when things went very badly wrong, nearly catastrophic. We came beam on twice into a rolling breaker, and she just went over. Both knockdowns happened in the space of half an hour. Not a half hour I ever want to repeat, I promise you! Nothing I could do, but I knew she'd pop right up again.

Kitty 4 is a real star, a real life saver, all the blokes in the boatyard should be so so proud of her. Wish you could have seen how she was lifting herself up out of the water, giving two fingers to the storm and the wind and the waves, like she was saying teeheehee you can't sink me. She was magnificent, awesome. And do you know the best thing? When I looked up through the cabin window after each knockdown was over, there was my albatross up there like he was on angel wings hovering over me, protecting me. We make a pretty good team, him and me. Managed to take a piccie of him with Mrs Betts' brilliant camera just when the storm was dying down. Sending it to you and Dr Topolski. When the worst was over, I managed to cook myself my first hot meal in two days, bacon and sausages and baked beans, a whole plateful — it was so yummy so good — and washed it all down with a mug of hot chocolate — of course. Still frozen in my fingers and feet, but I can feel a warm glow inside me now which wasn't there before. Love you loads. Allie.

2112hrs 3 April 38' 54"S 46' 03"W

Hi everyone. Tootling (Dad loved that word) along 5 knots. gentle swell. Phew. Got some time now to tell you bout Dr Topolski. We've emailed each other twice now, and we've spoken again too and we've seen one another at night at the same time. Here's how it happened. Dr Topolski phoned from the ISS and said they were passing over my position and could I see them. I went up on deck and there it was. He wanted me to shine a spotlight and put up a flare to see if they could see me. So I did and they saw me. Can you believe that, they really saw me. I could see him, he could see me. I could hear him — he could hear me — we laughed like a couple of kids, not cos it was funny but cos it was just amazing, amazing.

In his emails he has been telling me about the space walk, EVA he calls it, he's got to do in a couple of days. Never done one before and he was really looking forward to it. He's got to carry out some kind of scientific experiment. He told me a little of what it was about, but I didn't understand it really — didn't tell him that!

He's up there with a Russian physicist, Dr Uri Malakov and another American, Mike Petersen, he's the commander. The three of them have been up there nearly four weeks. Very cramped living quarters, that's what he told me. "I guess that's what you'd kind of expect in a Space Station. But at least we can fly about a bit whenever we feel like it. Weightlessness is the best, when you've gotten used to it."

He's told me a lot about himself, he's got a wife back home in Vermont and a couple of kids, ten and twelve, both girls. He's a scientist, a physicist, as well as an astronaut, pretty brainy sort of bloke, I'd say. I've been telling him a whole lot about us on my emails to him, about Dad and our trip to England to find Kitty. He's really interested, said he'd do anything he could to help, and I think he means it too. Decided he sounds more like Johnny Depp than George Clooney, but I've got his pic. He doesn't look like either. Looks more like Tom Hanks, got a kind face, a good face. He said he loved my emails and pics, specially the one of my albatross. He reckons we've got so much in common, each of us circumnavigating the earth in our own way, each of us in a tin can not exactly built for comfort. I told him he's doing his circumnavigation just a little faster than me, and he's got wide wide space around him and I've got wide wide sea.

He says my albatross is the most beautiful bird he's ever seen. That's one thing he misses up in space, he says, you look out of the window and you never see any birds. He wants me to send him a lot more pics of birds, so I will. He's emailed me some brilliant shots of the earth — we do live on such an awesome amazing planet. I've got lots of pics too of him floating about in his space station with Uri and Mike. So cool. Have to do that one day. He's got more room up there than I have down here but he's got to share it. Nice pics of him and his wife too, she's called Marianne, and his two kids in the snow outside their home. He looks like his voice, kind, thoughtful, intelligent. Hope his EVA goes well.

Fishing's been good today. I caught six and kept two for myself. Threw the rest to my albatross, my lip-smacking albatross. Every day he stays with me I know is a bonus. I shall so miss him when he goes, but I keep telling myself that this far north he can't stay around much longer and I'd better get myself ready for the day he's not there any more. No more news about Kitty then? She's got to be somewhere, right? See you. A xxx

1216hrs 5 April (GPS on the blink for some reason, so not sure of precise position)

Hello from the Atlantic. It's me again. Dr Topolski's sent me an email all about his EVA. He sounded so excited. Said Uri took lots of pics of him doing his slow-motion space dance. He'll send them on down when he can. Here's part of his email:

"I was six hours out there in space. I was busy, but I had plenty of time to look around me. That was when I guess I really understood for the first time the immensity of space, and the timelessness of it, the stillness of it. And our planet seemed to be suddenly so precious, so utterly beautiful. I thought of my family down in green Vermont, and of you out there on that blue, blue sea."

I emailed him back asking him why he did it, why he'd become an astronaut in the first place. He said it was all Neil Armstrong's fault, the first man on the moon. When he was little he'd sat there in front of his TV watching him step down on the moon's surface. Said it was listening to him speak from the moon that did it for him. "One small step for man, one giant leap for mankind." He'd wanted to go into space ever since, and he was loving it, except he could do with a little more privacy he said.

We sent emails back and forth comparing notes really. I'm down here at sea level, (well ground level), only the sea keeps moving so it's not level, and he's up 350km above ground. They're going at 5 miles a second up there in space. I'm doing 5 nautical miles an hour down here. I've got my laptop, my five GPSs (two of them are still on the blink) and some basic software. He's got all the most amazing gizmos in the world, most of it operated from NASA. He's floating around up there, I'm being bashed about down here. Don't tell him this, but I've decided I'm definitely better off down here. Except for his space walk, he's been shut in up in his space station for weeks. And at least I can breathe good clean sea air, and to be honest, I couldn't live in such a confined space for so long – I'd go bananas. I mean you couldn't even talk to yourself without being overheard could you? And he's got another month cooped up up there. Think I'll stick to sailing. But we're both adventurers, he said, both explorers, and just about the luckiest people alive because we're out there doing what we love best. "Isn't that great?" he said. He's right. It is great. I am lucky. He asked after Kitty, after my albatross, about the weather, about how I'm doing down here. He says it's hard to imagine how life must be for me, but he wants to know all about it says he wants to see diagrams of my yacht, inside and out. So I'll send them soon as I can. When he passed over I let off a flare again, but he couldn't see it this time. He's become a real friend to me, like no other. A friend I've never met.

Can now wiggle my little finger again Mum. So I've got all ten in use again now. Hands still sore, but otherwise I'm fit as a fiddle another Dad-ism. Why is a fiddle fit? Always wondered that.

There's some flying fish around, the first I've seen. My albatross doesn't seem at all interested in them. He's sitting there now waiting for me to put my line over the side again. I'll do it right now. Got to keep him happy, haven't I?

1202hrs 11 April 28' 54"S 44' 53"W

Hi Mum, Grandpa. Haven't heard from the ISS for a few days. Hope all's well with Dr Topolski up there. More flying fish about. Getting closer to the Tropics all the time. Feel like I'm being boiled alive down here. A month or so ago I couldn't feel my feet and fingers, now I'm sitting here pouring sweat. I want to open the hatch but I can't because the spray comes in and soaks everything. So I wear very little, only way. Visibility is v. poor. Brazilian coast to port, but I'm keeping well away from it, much as I'd love to see it. Lots of fishing boats out there. Can't sleep in this heat either — above 30. can't wait to get further north into the cold again. When I'm hot I want to be cold. When I'm cold I want to be hot. What's the matter with me? Still all of it will be worth it if we can find out where Kitty is. As I get closer — and I am getting closer now — I think about it more and more. I hope for it more and more. I keep looking at her key, Dad's key, keep wondering what it's for. GPS up and running again.

1520 14 April 25' 85"S 41' 31"W

The worst thing that could happen has happened, the saddest thing since Dad died. And it was me that did it. I should have known. I should have thought. My albatross is dead and I killed him. I didn't mean to, but that doesn't make me any less guilty, does it? I came up into the cockpit at dawn and looked around for my albatross as I always do. And he wasn't there. My heart sank because I always knew that one morning, I'd find him gone. I saw there were a few flying fish lying in the scuppers. I think that's what reminded me to check the fishing line. I could see at once the line was taut, so I thought I'd caught a fish. It wasn't a fish I'd caught, it was my albatross. He was being dragged along astern of the boat, hooked and drowned. I pulled him in and sat with him sodden and limp on my lap, his great wings stilled for ever. Mum, he came with me all this way and I've killed him, I've killed my albatross. but I've done something a lot worse than that. It's not just the albatross whose wings I've stilled. I feel deep in my heart that I've stilled Dad's spirit too. A.

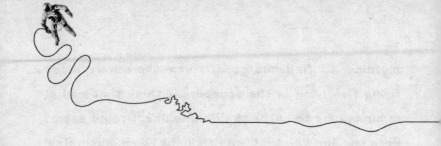

Alone on a Wide Wide Sea

It was only in the days and weeks following the killing of
my albatross that I understood what Dad really meant in
his story when he said that his "centre would not hold". I
know only from the emails I sent home each day after this
that I sailed north for a month. I think I must have sailed
on almost as if I was in a trance. It was like I was on
automatic pilot. I sailed efficiently. To get as far north as I
did, I must have done. I did everything that had to be
done, but I did it with no excitement, no joy, felt no fear
and no pain, not even any grief. I was numb. I just sailed
the boat. I told them I wanted the *Kitty Four* website down
for good. I recorded only my daily longitude and latitude
position. I didn't want to have any communications with

anyone any more. I ignored all the pleading emails that came in and I didn't answer the Satphone either. There was nothing more I wanted to say to anyone. I no longer cared about Kitty or the key. I no longer cared about anything. I even ignored all the messages of sympathy and encouragement that came in from Dr Topolski up in the ISS.

After ten days or so I did send one email that wasn't just longitude and latitude. Looking back now I'm not sure quite why I did it, unless it was an attempt to explain my silence to everyone at home, and up there in space. Maybe I couldn't find any words of my own, but I think it was more than that. By now I knew all of *The Ancient Mariner* so well. The words echoed in my head without my even wanting them to be there. Sometimes I'd just find myself sitting in the cockpit and the words and the lines would speak themselves out loud. And the more I recited it the more I lost myself in it, and came to believe that I was in some way the *Ancient Mariner*, that my journey, like his, was cursed because of what I'd done. Here's some of what I emailed on 28th April:

And I had done a hellish thing,
And it would work 'em woe:
For all averred, I had killed the bird
That made the breeze to blow.
Ah wretch! said they, the bird to slay,
that made the breeze to blow!

...Water, water, every where
And all the boards did shrink;
Water water, everywhere,
Nor any drop to drink.

I know now of course how worried everyone must have
been at home when they read this. I know now Grandpa
wanted to call the whole thing off, to mobilise a major air–sea
rescue at once to pick me up. But Mum had stood firm. And
the only reason she had stood firm was that she could see my
reports were still coming in each day. She could see on the
chart that I was making good progress on my journey north.
I know too that Dr Topolski was in close touch with them

during my long silence, and encouraged Mum in her decision to give me time to work things out on my own.

I still don't understand why I came out of the darkness of my despair when I did. We can't ever really know these things, I suppose. For Dad it was the moment when a nurse was kind to him in hospital in Hobart when he was at his lowest ebb, and helped him through. But even so he wouldn't have come out of his black hole unless he had really wanted to. If there was such a moment of revelation for me, the moment I found I wanted to start living again, I know exactly when it was, the exact day, the exact place it happened.

I was in the cockpit of *Kitty Four* when I saw him. A turtle. A leatherback turtle. He surfaced right beside the boat, and just swam along with me. He looked at me quizzically like he was asking me what I was doing there. I told him I was going to England to find Kitty. I told him everything, and he stayed and listened. I wasn't alone. I heard myself singing aloud in the wind. I hadn't sung for weeks. I went through my whole repertoire from *London Bridge* to *Here Comes the Sun* to *What a Wonderful World* to *I*

Will Always Love You, and I belted out the last one with tears pouring down my cheeks. When I'd finished, the turtle gave me one last look and left. I didn't mind. I hadn't cried ever since my albatross died. Something was gathering inside me, finding itself again, during these songs. It was my centre.

Maybe keeping myself as busy as I had been with the sailing was the best therapy I could have had to lift me out of the sadness I had been living through. Maybe also it was because I could see that the end of my journey was in sight now. I was only 2500 miles and twenty-three days out from Falmouth. But one thing I'm quite sure of. That day sitting there talking to the turtle, singing and crying in the cockpit of *Kitty Four*, I felt I was not alone any more. Mum was there with me, Grandpa, Dr Topolski, everyone at home, and Dad too. They were all there with me, willing me on. There was still grief in those tears I cried, but it was a sudden surge of joy that had released them.

I went down into the cabin then to email home at once, and I saw there was an email waiting for me from Dr Topolski. He was back on earth now. They'd brought him down a week before, in Kazakhstan, a bit of a bumpy landing, he said, and he was back home with his family now on leave for a while, and he'd been doing some investigations. He hadn't forgotten about me. On the contrary, he'd been in touch with Mum and Grandpa a lot ever since he got down. He'd come up with something "pretty interesting" about Kitty, but, tantalisingly, he wouldn't say what it was. He did tell me that his whole family knew about me, that they were all thinking of me every day, that they had a map of the Atlantic ocean pinned up on the kitchen wall and were charting my progress, moving the bright yellow pin that was me a little further north and little closer to England every morning. He knew that I'd been going through a hard time, he said, but he wanted me to know, "There's a whole bunch of people here in Vermont and all over the world just rooting for you." Every day after that I felt as if I was recharging myself somehow.

I was sailing into trade winds which didn't make for comfortable sailing, but I didn't mind. It wasn't only the winds that were blowing us along now anyway – and *Kitty*

Four was flying – it was the emails that came in all the time from everyone at home, and from Dr Topolski too, everyone contributing to my new sense of wellbeing, of euphoria almost. I never saw my turtle again, but I've never forgotten him. I can still see his face gazing up at me, a kind face, old and wise. Sometimes I think that turtle saved my life.

With every day that brought me closer to England, I kept asking them about Kitty, but all I got back was that there was no real news. They had one or two hopeful "irons in the fire", whatever that meant. It didn't sound very hopeful. To be honest, I thought they were just stringing me along, trying to keep my spirits up, knowing perfectly well that the last thing I needed to hear was bad news about Kitty – that they couldn't find any trace of her, or worse, that they had discovered she was dead. Often I'd sit there down in the cabin, Dad's lucky key cupped in my hand, wondering what had been so important about this key. What did it mean? Why had Kitty given it to Dad that day all those years before when they were parted? What was so special about it? He had always called it his lucky key. I'd hold it and squeeze it tight, and every time I'd wish on it, just as Dad used to wish on it. I wished I'd find Kitty alive and well in England and that I'd find out at last what the key was for.

I'd be lying if I said that my new euphoria didn't from time to time give way to times of sadness. There was still an ache inside me, left by the loss of my albatross, that would not go away. I thought of him so often. Every bird I saw reminded me of him, of the majesty of his flight, of his grace and his beauty. And sitting in my cockpit in a cold grey North Atlantic, I looked out and saw an albatross of a different kind, an albatross of the north, a gannet, diving down to fish, splicing the sea. He was magnificent, but not as magnificent as my albatross.

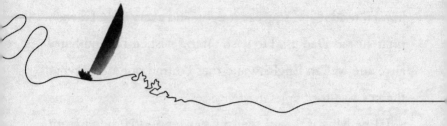

"London Bridge is Falling Down"

It was a good thing I was so buoyed up now and so determined, because in those last couple of thousand miles just about everything that could go wrong did go wrong. First of all, the North Atlantic turned out to be every bit as vicious and hostile as the Southern Ocean. *Kitty Four* took a terrible battering. And it wasn't just one storm, it was a whole succession of them. We'd sail out of one and straight into another. We got knocked down three times in three days, and the last time was very nearly the end of the story.

Not many single-handed sailors go over the side and live to tell the tale. I did. It was my own fault it happened. As Dad used to say, I was a silly chump. I was in the cockpit in a storm and I wasn't harnessed in properly. Yes, I was tired. I hadn't slept for a couple of days. But that's no excuse. I was just a chump and very nearly a dead chump. I was caught completely unawares when the wave came. As the boat lurched violently I was catapulted overboard. Somehow I managed to grab a safety wire and just clung on to it. But *Kitty Four* was on her side and I was dunked in the ocean. I remember hearing the roar of the sea in my ears, and I knew that was always the last sound a drowning sailor ever hears. Then *Kitty Four* righted herself. She flipped up and I found myself flung back into the cockpit still in one piece, just. But I was nursing a broken arm – I knew it was broken at once because it was completely useless – and I was cursing myself loudly. You're a lucky chump, a very lucky chump, I thought, when I'd stopped my cursing. My survival was down to Dad's key, I had no doubt about it, it was entirely down to Dad's lucky key.

I didn't feel any pain in my arm at first. It was too cold after my dunking in the freezing waters of the North Atlantic. But when I'd dried off and warmed up down below in the cabin, then it began to hurt like hell. I knew I'd need help, so I picked up the Satphone and rang home. Grandpa answered. I told him all I needed was a doctor to tell me what to do, and I'd manage. No arguments, Grandpa said, he was going to have me airlifted off. "You can't sail a boat with a broken arm," he said. I don't think I'd ever shouted at Grandpa before (or since) but I did now. I told him that we were only fifty miles or so off the coast of England, off the Scilly Isles, which was less than a hundred miles from Falmouth; that *Kitty Four* and I were going to finish this thing together, and that I'd never speak to him again if he did it. Mum and Grandpa had a little talk about it – and five minutes later I had Dr Topolski on the phone. It turned out he was a doctor of medicine as well as a doctor of physics and engineering and just about everything else. He "examined" me by asking me dozens of questions. Then he talked me through how to make a splint, how to bandage it to my arm – not easy one-handed, but I did it.

Of course it wasn't just me that was beaten up and hurting. It was *Kitty Four* too. Not the boat herself, she was fine. She'd just rocked and rolled, and bobbed up again, like she always did. She'd been built to be indestructible and unsinkable, and she was. It was all the bits and pieces that were beginning to fail as we neared the English Channel. Neither the generator nor the desalinator was reliable any more. The self-steering was in pieces. I'd tried mending it, but with one arm I couldn't do it, so it meant I had to be up there in the cockpit almost all the time. In fact I'd have had to be there anyway, because there was a lot of shipping about now, more than I'd had on the whole trip, and for a little yacht, for any yacht, that's dangerous. I could see them, but in seas like this I'd be lucky if they saw me before they ran me down.

I didn't tell anyone how bad things were really getting. I knew how Grandpa would react, how upset Mum would be. Instead I wrote chirpy emails, sounded deliberately upbeat and jokey on the Satphone. I think maybe that having to sound chirpy was very good for me. The truth was that I was now really worried that I might not be able to make it. My arm pained me every time I moved. Every sail change I made was sheer agony. I came to a decision.

I emailed home saying I'd put into Scilly, and not go on to Falmouth. After all Scilly was England. It was as good a port as any to end the first half of my voyage. Mum phoned me back. She said she and Grandpa had thought about it and they were flying over to England as soon as possible, and they would let me know when they'd landed. I said I didn't want any fuss, and that they weren't to tell anyone what had happened. I was already dreading a welcoming flotilla coming out to meet me. Grandpa said that even with no website up there, there was huge interest in the papers everywhere.

"Just don't tell them I'm coming into Scilly," I told him. "Promise me, Grandpa." He promised, but I wasn't convinced. I knew the temptation of having "Stavros Boats" on the television news in big letters, and his little Allie, the apple of his Greek eye, standing on deck and waving, would be too much to resist. To be honest I expected the worst, but I'd come to terms with it. Maybe it would be quite fun anyway, and even if I didn't like it, I could stand back and smile through gritted teeth – after all, I'd done that before in Hobart.

So there we were the next day tootling along with a bit of a limp, but happy as Larry (I do sound like Dad sometimes I know, but I love the phrases he used. I inherited them. They're mine now.) All the storms were behind us. The forecast was set fair all the way to Scilly. Sunshiney day, clear skies, and not a sign of a welcoming flotilla – amazing, Grandpa had kept quiet. I had just sighted land, not much land, but land all the same, and it was the land I wanted to see – the Scilly Islands. I toasted the occasion with a mug of hot chocolate. The Scillies looked like little grey dumplings lying there low in the sea, about ten miles off. We were going nicely, about five knots. It was early morning. I was so nearly there. I'd seen a whale, or perhaps a basking shark, in the distance the day before and was looking out for him again. What I saw instead was a school of porpoises playing off my starboard bow, giving me quite a show. This was the kind of unexpected, spontaneous welcome I really wanted.

But I was enjoying it so much that I wasn't keeping a good look-out all around. That was when a sickening shudder shook the boat. She reared up and rolled, and then crashed down into the sea, where she stopped dead, as if the life had suddenly gone out of her. The tiller was light in my hand, so I knew at once that we'd lost the rudder. Then I saw pieces of it floating away astern of us. I thought at first we must have hit the whale, but we hadn't. The dark shape I saw lurking just beneath the surface rose then and showed itself. It was a dirty orange with flat sides and sharp edges. A container, a lousy stinking container. I cursed that container ship wherever she was, then I cursed all container ships wherever they were. Cursing over, I checked below. At least we weren't holed. We hadn't lost buoyancy. We were rudderless and helpless, but still afloat. I hoped we could drift in on the tide at first, but a quick look at my chart confirmed what I already knew, that there were rocks all around Scilly, thousands and thousands of them.

I had no choice. I used the Satphone and called out the lifeboat. Within half an hour they were alongside and threw me a line. So with a busted rudder and a busted arm I arrived on the Scilly Isles, came into St Mary's Harbour, towed in ignominiously by the lifeboat. Because of that, of course, there was a lot of interest, and very soon they found out who I was. No flotilla, thank goodness, but any hope I might have had of slipping in unnoticed was gone. They whisked me up to the hospital to have my arm looked at and told me I had to stay there the night, but I said I didn't want to. I'd had a better offer. Matt Pender, the lifeboat coxswain, said he could put me up at home with his family. So after my arm was set and plastered he came to fetch me, and we went straight to a pub where they fêted me as if I was Ellen McArthur. "Proper little hero" they called me. Everyone made a fuss of me and I loved it. I tried phoning home, but no one answered. They'd probably left already. I didn't mind. I was so happy to have got to England, so happy the boat was in one piece, just about.

I did some TV and radio interviews the next day, got them over with. Then I went down to the jetty to tidy *Kitty Four* before she went off for repairs. There were crowds all around her, dozens of people photographing her, and she was just bobbing up and down loving it all, taking her bows.

I waited about till everyone had gone before I went on board. Then we had a quiet time together, just *Kitty Four* and me. I emailed Mum, emailed Dr Topolski, told everyone that repairs would take a couple of weeks at least, that I would catch the ferry the following day from Scilly to Penzance, and then the night train to London Paddington getting in at seven o'clock on the Wednesday morning. If they were there by then, they could meet me, and we could go off to Bermondsey and start looking for Kitty right away. I told them something else too, something I knew neither of them would want to hear. I'd decided that once *Kitty Four* was repaired, once my arm was better, I would be sailing *Kitty Four* home. I'd do the whole thing just as I'd planned, the whole circumnavigation, and nothing anyone could say would stop me. "I mean it, Grandpa," I wrote. Before I left *Kitty Four* I got an email back.

"Whatever you say, Allie. See you at Paddington seven a.m. Wednesday morning. There's a big clock there on platform one. Meet you there. Love Mum and Grandpa." They'd given in just like that. I couldn't believe it.

Matt and the whole lifeboat crew came to see me off on the ferry to Penzance. I'd never been hugged so much in all my life. I liked it, I liked it a lot. I had to wait around a while until I could get on the night train for London. So I was quite tired by the time I got into my seat. I was getting out my laptop. I wanted to send another email to Mum. When I looked up, there was this bloke sitting opposite smiling at me. We got talking as you do. His name was Michael McLuskie.

The rest you know already, just about all of it, anyway. What you don't know is what happened when I'd finished telling him my story, when we got into Paddington Station the next morning. The train came into platform one, and we got out together, Michael carrying my rucksack as well as his. (He wasn't just good-looking, he was thoughtful too, still is – mostly.) I could see Mum and Grandpa under the clock waiting, looking around for me.

"That them?" Michael asked.

"That's them," I said.

"So it's true, all if it, everything you told me. None of it made up?"

"None of it."

"Then," he said, looking straight at me, and meaning every word he said, "then you are the most incredible person I've ever met, and I'd like to see you again, if that's alright."

I don't know to this day what made me say it. "Look," I said. "I'm hungry. Why don't you come and have breakfast with us, with Mum and Grandpa and me?" He didn't say no, which was why, after Mum and Grandpa had each hugged me again and again, and after we'd all cried and laughed Cretan style under the clock at Paddington, we all piled into a taxi, and went off to their hotel for breakfast.

They seemed, I thought, a little nervous. Grandpa kept looking away whenever I caught his eye. I thought he was cross with me because I'd insisted on doing the whole circumnavigation. He'd always been so much against it. Mum couldn't seem to find her voice at all, just sat there patting my hand fondly. I exchanged glances with Michael who shrugged with his eyes, as only he can do.

It was one of those huge modern hotels, made entirely of

glass, and was right on the river. We walked into the breakfast room which was full of laid up tables, all of them empty except for a large round table near the window. Sitting around it were what looked like a family with a couple of kids and all of them were looking at me very intently, which was odd, I thought. And Mum and Grandpa weren't leading us to one of the empty tables, as I expected they would. Instead they were leading us directly towards the round one by the window. "And this," Mum said to them, not trying to disguise the pride in her voice, "this is Allie, my daughter Allie. Arthur's daughter, Allie."

Still they stared, and then, one by one the stares turned to smiles. "I think you had better introduce yourselves," Mum went on.

"Shall I start?" I knew who he was before he opened his mouth. I recognised him from his photograph. "I'm Marc, Marc Topolski. From up there, remember? And this is my family, Marianne, Molly and Martha, known in the neighbourhood back home in Vermont as the M&Ms." I couldn't speak, partly because I was so choked up. But there was another reason too.

Even as he was talking, I was looking at the old lady sitting next to him. Her smile was Dad's smile, from the eyes, from the heart.

"And I'm Kitty," she said. "Your dad's sister."

She could hardly speak either, but smiled through her tears. "You got Arthur's key, dear?" she said. "The one I gave him?" I took it off from around my neck and gave it to her. There was a small wooden box on the table in front of her, carved and painted with red and white flowers. She turned the key in the lock. It fitted. She smiled up at me again. She turned it, then she went on turning it, again and again, which seemed strange. Then she opened the lid, and I understood everything. The box played music. It was a musical box. And the tune it played was *London Bridge is Falling Down*. We listened until it slowed right down, and then finished mid-tune.

"And that," said the old lady pointing out at the river, and I noticed now that she too had a kind of American accent, "that is London Bridge, and it isn't falling down. I was born just down the road in Bermondsey. It's where your dad was born too. My mother and father were killed in a bombing raid in the war. This musical box was all that was left of our home. We were in the same orphanage together, Arthur and me. We loved listening to this, over and over. We'd listen to it for hours. Then they took your dad away. I gave him the key, and I told him I wouldn't play our tune again until he brought the key back. Then I would wind it up for him and we would listen to it together – I was the eldest you see, I always did the winding up. I never heard it again until today. It's yours now, Allie. And if you have children one day, then maybe you'll pass it on to them, and you'll tell them the story of how in the end the key found the musical box and the musical box found the key."

I was still unable to make sense of it all. "But how did they find you?" I asked. "I don't understand."

"That was your astronaut friend here," said my Aunty Kitty. "He went on television in the US when he came down from his space travels and told the whole world about you, this amazing eighteen-year-old girl from Australia called Allie Hobhouse, sailing single-handedly around the world on a little boat called *Kitty Four*, sailing all the way to England to find her father's long lost sister to fulfil a promise she'd made to her father on his death bed. The father, he said, was called Arthur Hobhouse, his sister, Kitty Hobhouse. Anyone who can help, phone in. So I did. You see, when they sent your dad off to Australia all those years ago, a lifetime ago, they sent me to Canada. I got lucky. I landed up with a lovely family in Niagara-On-the-Lake. I live there still right by the shore in the same house I was brought up in. You must come and see it sometime."

I noticed then a copy of Dad's story in front of her, right by her bowl of cornflakes.

"Have you read it yet?" I asked.

"I only just got it," she said. "Trouble is, my eyes aren't very good at reading any more. Maybe you could read it to me after breakfast."

So that's what I did, an hour or so later. I read it to them, sitting there overlooking London Bridge and the Thames.

*   *   *

"'The story of Arthur Hobhouse'," I began. "'Arthur Hobhouse is a happening. I should begin at the beginning, I know that. But the trouble is, I don't know the beginning. I wish I did...'"

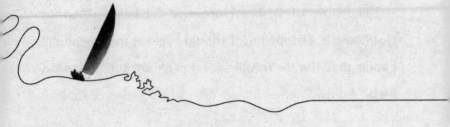

Now you've read the book

Now you've read the book, I want you to know something. The two stories we wrote were never intended to be published. We each of us wrote our story simply as a record of what had happened, first to my father, Arthur Hobhouse, and then to me. I thought long and hard about whether to publish. This is after all a family story. How much you tell the world about your family is a delicate matter for everyone concerned. But the family is happy about it, as I am, because our stories, Dad's and mine, had already been acted out in public, to some extent at least. And certainly, had this not happened, our story could not possibly have ended as well as it did. In other words our private family story was never totally private in the first place. It was in the newspapers, on the radio, on television. But the whole of our story has never been fully told. And that's why we all thought that it should be. Dad would have wanted it, I know, because he believed that we live on only as long as our story is told. I believe that too.

Afterword

It is estimated that between 1947 and 1967 somewhere between 7000 and 11,000 British children were sent to Australia alone.

It was at one time thought convenient to pack up your troublesome people, whether they were convicts or simply unwanted or orphaned children, and ship them off to what were then the colonies – mostly Canada, New Zealand and Australia.

The first white Australians were convicts settled there forcibly in 1788. It was a form of banishment.

The banishment of children, which went on for centuries and reached its modern peak in the years after the Second World War, was in many ways just as cruel, but it was sometimes well meant. Children who had nothing could be provided with a new land, a new family, some prospects of living a happy life, away from the seething slums of Britain's cities. And many of them did get lucky, landed up in the right place with genuinely kind people who looked after them and cared for them. However just as many did not. One former child migrant said, "Most of us have been left with broken hearts and broken lives."* Cruelty, abuse and exploitation were tragically all too common.

Another wrote this:

"For the vast majority of former child migrants the most often asked question is 'Who am I?' Most of us were born in the British Isles of British parents. Our culture, heritage and traditions are British. Our nationality, our rights and our privileges were our inheritance. Unable to make a reasoned decision we were transported 20,000 kilometres to the other side of the world. Our crime for the most part was that we were the children of broken relationships. Our average age was eight years and nine months. In this one act, we were stripped of our parents and our brothers and sisters. We were stripped of our grandparents and extended families. We were stripped of nationality, culture and birthright. Many of us were stripped of our family name and even our birth date. We were stripped of our personhood, human rights and our dignity. We were referred to as migrant boy number 'so and so' or migrant girl number 'so and so'. And so we arrived, strangers in a lost land, lost and with no way back."*

It was because of harrowing accounts like this that I wrote my story.

Michael Morpurgo

* Source: The House of Commons Health Select Committee's report On the Welfare of Former British Child Migrants, 1998

If you or your family are interested in locating a former child migrant, or you are a former migrant seeking your family, you can obtain a document describing the available resources (including a contact database and financial support) from the UK Department of Health.

As a clickable file:

http://www.dh.gov.uk/assetRoot/04/09/00/30/04090030.pdf

As a text-only file:

http://www.dh.gov.uk/assetRoot/04/09/00/31/04090031.pdf